BIRMINGHAM:
NOT A PLACE TO PROMISE MUCH

Also available in this series:

Fred Archer	THE DISTANT SCENE
	THE SECRETS OF BREDON HILL
H. E. Bates	THE VANISHED WORLD
	FLYING BOMBS OVER ENGLAND
Adrian Bell	CORDUROY
Margaret Bramford	FROM COTTAGE TO PALACE
Brenda Bullock	A POCKET WITH A HOLE
Mary Craddock	A NORTH COUNTRY MAID
Vivienne Draper	THE CHILDREN OF DUNSEVERICK
Denis Farrier	COUNTRY VET
Lady Fortescue	BEAUTY FOR ASHES
	RETURN TO "SUNSET HOUSE"
	TRAMPLED LILIES
Mollie Harris	ANOTHER KIND OF MAGIC
Janet Hitchman	THE KING OF THE BARBAREENS
Grace Horseman	GROWING UP IN THE FORTIES
Rachel Knappett	A PULLET ON THE MIDDEN
Brian P. Martin	TALES OF THE OLD VILLAGERS
Frank Moore	
and John Hynam	THE HORSES KNEW THE WAY
John Moore	THE BLUE FIELD
	BRENSHAM VILLAGE
	PORTRAIT OF ELMBURY
Phyllis Nicholson	COUNTRY BOUQUET
Barbara Paynter	THE GRASS WIDOW AND HER COW
Humphrey Phelps	JUST AROUND THE CORNER
Geoffrey Robinson	HEDINGHAM HARVEST
Stephen Rynne	GREEN FIELDS
Edward Storey	THE WINTER FENS
Joyce Storey	JOYCE'S WAR
Pat Warner	LOCK KEEPER'S DAUGHTER
Doreen Louie West	LOUIE: A COUNTRY LADY
Hazel Wheeler	THE MILLINER'S APPRENTICE
Roderick Wilkinson	MEMORIES OF MARYHILL

BIRMINGHAM:

NOT A PLACE TO PROMISE MUCH

Reflections on life in the city between the two World Wars

Written by
Donald Pigott

ISIS
LARGE PRINT
Oxford, England

Copyright © Donald Pigott 1997

First published in Great Britain 1997
by Brewin Books

Published in Large Print 1998 by ISIS Publishing Ltd,
7 Centremead, Osney Mead, Oxford OX2 0ES,
by arrangement with Brewin Books

British Library Cataloguing in Publication Data
Pigott, Donald
  Birmingham: not a place to promise much. – Large print ed.
  – (Reminiscence series)
  1. Pigott, Donald 2. Large type books 3. Birmingham (England)
  – Social life and customs
  I. Title
  942.4'96'085'092

                    ISBN 0-7531-5449-8

Printed and bound by MPG Books Ltd, Bodmin, Cornwall

To my son Nigel, for his patience and help with computer technology

CONTENTS

PROLOGUE

"They came from Birmingham, which is not a place to promise much. One has not great hopes from Birmingham. I always say there is something direful in the sound."

Mrs Elton in Jane Austen's Emma

"I want to go to Birmingham". The ticket clerk at Euston peered through his window at the young lady who spoke from the booking hall beyond. His lips curled into a wry smile. "You mean you *have* to go to Birmingham," he replied, sliding a cardboard ticket and the change from a one pound note towards her.

The incident may be of doubtful authenticity. Only a reckless employee would have had the temerity to address an intending passenger so imprudently in 1930, when attempted levity could have been misconstrued as impertinence with a risk of dismissal into a world of depression and unemployment. It does, however, convey with startling clarity an outsider's dismal impression of a city that was dull, uninteresting and lacking in culture. The citizens of Birmingham would have been quick to refute this, but the impression was not entirely without foundation.

A novel one-way traffic system, where some of the trams proceeded in a direction contrary to the main flow of traffic, had recently been introduced and had turned the city into a motorist's nightmare and a topic for music hall jokes. The city's architecture; mock Gothic spires, turrets and pinnacles, Italianate domes and balustrades, had become so encrusted with smoke, grime and pigeon droppings, that it was difficult to imagine how they had looked in their prime. The Corinthian columns of the Town Hall were becoming dangerously eroded and the stones of the Council House were so blackened that, as children, we thought it might have been built from lumps of coal. The smoke from thousands of domestic and factory chimneys descended continuously from heavily-laden skies, threatening health, damaging buildings and ruining clothes. Smokeless zones lay years away and legislation leading to clean air acts was beyond prophecy. They were not even contemplated, and all the discomforts of an unhealthy environment were accepted as inevitable.

The citizens, always ready to respond to falling fortunes in one trade by changing to another, were not unduly perturbed by the dreary image of their city. They had far more important things to think about. Most of them worked for low wages in factories that had grown out of misery, and the enforced nationwide reduction in wages was causing great anxiety. The depression had thrown thousands out of work and put many more on short time, making them apprehensive of the future.

There was little money to spare and any pleasures were few and simple. Many families rarely, if ever, left the confines of their immediate neighbourhood. Hardly anyone owned a car, nor did they ever expect to own one, any more than they contemplated owning a house, shares in a company, or a holiday abroad. A holiday even in this country was the privilege of the few not the expectation of everyone. For the majority, Birmingham in the early 1930s did not promise much. For most their greatest hopes were for an occasional tram ride into town to look at the shops and, perhaps, an annual outing to the Lickey Hills or a trip to Sutton Park. There were, nevertheless, many compensations and diversions, un-sophisticated though they were, and the Victorian city, which may not have been a thing of beauty, is affectionately remembered by those who grew up there between the two world wars.

In the 1930s the city centre was very compact. It was roughly bounded by Colmore Row, Bull Street, High Street and New Street. It was perhaps because it was so confined that it had a unique cosiness that was absent from other cities. Unchanged for almost a century, the familiar face of Birmingham had vanished for ever by 1970.

The city, with its obsession for cars and concrete, suffered more than most in the vast remaking. Much of that which had escaped wartime bombing was ruthlessly bulldozed into the ground in a frenzy of reconstruction. Old city streets that were once full of character and fascination were swept away to make room for the fly-overs and underpasses; only their names have been perpetuated in some of the ringways and circuses. People, now cocooned in cars, funnelled into gusty passages or forced onto escalators to stand like ranked robots, remotely-controlled and progressed mechanically, once thronged the narrow pavements. They overflowed into the congested roadways intermingling with trams, buses and horse-drawn and motor traffic in fierce competition for right of way.

Today a hot potato man still stands in Stephenson Place. His roasting machine is not the archaic contraption that once stood there; black with gleaming brass bands and a tall chimney reminiscent of the *Rocket*, but the fragrance that wafts from the machine instantly recalls the smells, the sights and sounds of bygone Birmingham. The intervening years evaporate and nostalgia usurps the contemporary scene.

From the lower end of Stephenson Place the acrid smell of a mixture of smoke, steam and oil from the locomotives straining beneath the vast glass roof of New Street Station again assails the nostrils. The hiss of escaping steam and the impatient shriek of an engine's whistle echo through the booking hall. At the corner of New Street and Corporation Street, outside the *Birmingham Mail* offices, newsboys shout "Spatchermyle" (*Despatch* or *Mail*) at a time when the city had two morning and two evening papers.

Further along Corporation Street the air resounds with the tram drivers' clanging gongs, impatient of the traffic that impedes their progress along inflexible tracks. Near the bus stop in Bull Street a wandering musician stands. A plaintive rendering of the "Miserere" from Verdi's *Il Trovatore* wails from his violin and is intermittently drowned by the harsh manual gear-changing from the petrol-driven buses and the shouts of the bus conductors' "Left inside, right on top" to speed the loading of their vehicles. The sad musician seems to have no other melody in his repertoire and his one doleful tune plays on the heartstrings and prevails on the pockets of the crowds surging in and out of Grey's department store.

From an alleyway, doubtless selected for its echoing properties, resounds the voice of an old crone imploring the passing throng to "Count your Blessings." Occasionally she varies her ballad with a rendition of *The Glory Song* or *The Volunteer Organist.* In contrast, at the confluence of the Midland and City arcades, a blind mendicant stands next to a legless matchseller who sits on a trolley; both offering their wares in silent pleading.

At the Snow Hill end of the Great Western Arcade is the most enthralling toyshop that ever enchanted the eyes of children. One of its windows is crammed with model yachts, lead soldiers, farm animals and performing acrobats. In another there are working models constructed from the latest Meccano sets, Hornby trains circling on tinplate tracks, Tudor houses built from Lott's real stone bricks, and tram conductors' uniforms with bell punch and ticket rack stitched onto a piece of card. Across the road, outside the station, old flower sellers in long black skirts, soiled pinafores and shapeless black hats, urge their blooms on the crowds that throng the station entrance or swarm, homeward bound, onto the tramcars converging on tracks from Livery Street and the Cathedral terminus.

In the deepening gloom of a winter Saturday the steep cobbled incline of the Bull Ring has its own atmosphere. Beneath the glare of the market traders' naphtha flares kerbside hawkers urge rolling beans, blow-out ticklers, monkeys on sticks and penny 'andy carriers on the jostling crowds.

There are no neon signs but there are intriguing electric light advertisements with bulbs that flash on and off conspiring to convey their messages. High above the Navigation Street tram terminus and on the end of New Street Station an illuminated outline of an LMS locomotive appears against the night sky. Its wheels begin to turn, the connecting rods move, the wheels revolve and puffs of smoke emerge from its chimney. A few seconds and the vision disappears to be repeated after a brief interval. A "blinking owl" advertises spectacles on the premises of Harrison's optician's shop at the top of Snow Hill and, on "Galloway's Corner", "Use Swan Pens" flashes across Victoria Square. All have gone: the buildings that supported them all demolished. Paradise may have been regained in the Circus that perpetuates its name but, for those of us who grew up in the city between the wars, it has been lost forever.

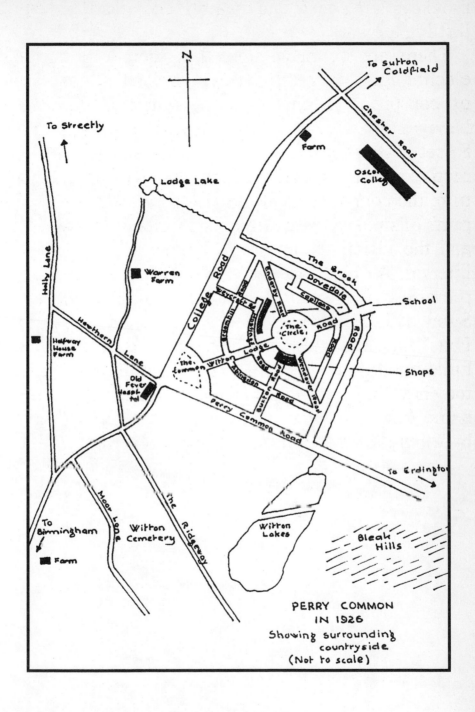

PERRY COMMON
IN 1926
Showing surrounding
countryside
(Not to scale)

Homes Fit For Heroes

On a May morning in 1926 an open lorry loaded with the barest essential furniture and household items sped northwards from Lozells along Birchfield Road. Sped, because although the contemporary unrest was not so evident in Birmingham as in London where armoured vehicles were patrolling the streets during the General Strike, the driver was anxious to leave the built-up area. My father, mother, my younger brother and I were crammed into the driver's cab, looking more like refugees fleeing the pursuit of some invading army than expectant tenants travelling to a new council housing estate that was being built on the northern periphery of the city, but there was no other way. Trams and buses had been abandoned in their depots and the new furniture that had been ordered remained undelivered in Lewis's warehouse. Just why we moved and managed to obtain transport at the height of the Strike remains a mystery.

The driver slackened his pace as we approached open country and trundled past the deserted tram terminus at Perry Barr. Beyond the bridge that crossed the LMS station there were few signs of civilisation. The freshly-emerged leaves on the trees, unsoiled by the dust and fumes from motor vehicles, glistened in the sunlight along the lane leading to the Zigzag Bridge; today a footpath, it was then the main highway. At the old

Boar's Head where the M6 Motorway now straddles a dual carriageway the lorry forked right past a farmstead and laboured up College Road to Perry Common, one of the highest points in the city. Here on a desolate tract of land exposed to the keen winds that swept over the aptly-named Bleak Hills, some of the "homes fit for heroes" promised by the politicians during the war that had ended eight years earlier were being built.

The Common had, in 1814, been one of the last to be enclosed, and the estate being built there was surrounded by fields and isolated from the city. The expanse of Witton Cemetery, Witton Lakes and the Bleak Hills formed a natural barrier to the South and effectively cut the estate off from the rest of the city. To the East a lane led past an occasional dwelling to Erdington village. Across the fields to the North Oscott College was silhouetted on the distant horizon and westward, as yet still in Staffordshire, open country stretched towards Walsall.

The small council estate, one of the first to be built after the late war, was bounded on two sides by College Road and Perry Common Road. Dovedale Road curved through a right angle governed by the course of a little brook to form the other two. The estate was characterised by a pattern of curved and straight roads. At its centre a circle of wasteland surrounded by undeveloped areas had been left vacant for the erection of shops and other amenities. All around were the vestiges of rural life where land was still farmed. At Warren Farm, Halfway House and Holford and Wellhead Farms cattle were milked, crops were harvested and sheep grazed tranquilly in the surrounding meadows.

Our new municipal house, as it was called, was opposite a school being built in Hastings Road. It gleamed with fresh paint and pebble dash rendering but, apart from a slight variation in its frontage, was identical to all the others. A tiny hall, from which the staircase ascended, led directly into the living room fitted with a picture rail and a dresser, its appearance marred by the intrusion of an ugly cast iron coal-burning range that was not even equipped to supply hot water.

From the rear of the room a door opened into a scullery that had the barest of facilities; a sink with a brass cold water tap and a cast iron gas stove. A pantry, a coal house and a bathroom led from the scullery. Another brass tap in the bathroom also supplied cold water but hot water for baths and for laundry had to be drawn off by the bucketful from a fuel-burning boiler that stood in the corner. There was no hand basin; one was expected to wash at the kitchen sink. It was a curiosity of the planning that the lavatory was outside and the coal house inside, with the unfortunate results that attention to human needs was delayed as long as possible during inclement weather and a rainsodden coalman dripped dirt across the scullery floor and filled the air with reeking coal dust. The living room coal fire supplied the only heating, but there had been a choice between gas or electric lighting. Most tenants chose the novelty of the latter although it promised to be more expensive. No power socket outlets were provided. We would have had no use for them.

Most of the new tenants; pioneers of the council house era had been waiting for years and living, as we had, in

3

cramped quarters with relatives or in lodgings. Many had become accustomed to sharing a lavatory and one cold water tap with others in a dismal courtyard. Running water, electric light, privacy, and a garden were luxuries and there were few objections to a weekly rent of eleven and sixpence (57p), although this represented a considerable part of a man's wages of between three and four pounds. We were among the first few tenants who had been carefully selected "better paid workers" who were able and willing to pay a "reasonable rent" which, coupled with increased living costs and travelling, placed council housing beyond the reach of the poor. My father must have been earning in excess of the three pounds ten shillings, which was considered to be the minimum to qualify as a "good tenant" of a council house.

It was some time before the awaited new furniture that had been saved for over many years, was delivered, lovingly polished and arranged. Books, china and ornaments that had lain in boxes were unpacked and displayed in what was to become our home for the next thirteen years.

The rent was collected by Mr Appleyard, a taciturn man with an authoritative air. Mr Appleyard did not live on the estate and no-one knew whence he came except that it was from the Estates Department. He arrived at precisely the same time every Monday morning and expected each door to be opened immediately in response to his peremptory knock. Mr Appleyard did not like to be kept waiting. He rarely entered a house, except to investigate a complaint, preferring to transact his business on the doorstep with the minimum of delay.

Everyone had a courteous regard for Mr Appleyard, for it was he who decided whether or not a sashcord needed attention or just how far a tenant might be allowed to fall into arrears before he reported the matter to the "Estates". He was also responsible for the maintenance and supervision of the estate. He cast an eye at the gardens to ensure that they were well kept. He glanced at the front garden hedges to make sure that the privet was well-trimmed and did not exceed the height stipulated, and it was a brave child who swung on a gate, climbed a lamp post or "chalked" on a fence when the "rent man" was around.

Most of the breadwinners on the estate worked on the production lines at the GEC, Fort Dunlop, Kynoch's (now IMI) where my father was employed as an engineer's turner. He had been engaged in making munitions during the war and was fortunate to be kept on afterwards when many were made redundant. Other men worked in the small factories in or around Witton, Aston or Perry Barr. There were some tram or bus drivers or conductors, bricklayers and semi-skilled workers employed in the growing motor industry, and a postman who wore a curiously-shaped helmet that resembled an inverted coal scuttle minus its handle.

There were a few "foreigners" who had been moved from London to work at Kynoch's and who spoke with an unfamiliar accent and sometimes used words that were strange to us. They were considerately housed in Weycroft Road which quickly became known as

5

"Cockneys Corner". There was one Scottish family and one Welsh. There were no ethnic minorities and, consequently, no integration or multi-racial problems. Such words would not have been understood. We were in a proud one-class society. The doctor, the dentist, curate, schoolteacher and others considered to be on higher rungs of the social ladder did not live on council estates.

By the standards of today we were all poor, but no-one was impoverished and none considered themselves to be underprivileged or disadvantaged. As "good tenants" we were all in what was quaintly termed the "respectable working class" in a rigid system unthinkable today and of which almost nothing remains. Why such a system continued after the Great War is not easy to understand, but people had been brought up to "know their places" in a pattern where there was little movement between the classes. Imprisoned in the system themselves many parents urged their children to better themselves. For most it was a hopeless dream. Lack of opportunity, apathy, prejudice even, closed the doors. Backsliding was rare. Hard work, privation and well-patched clothing prevented this. The respectable working classes did not wish to associate with rough vagrants, unpleasant beggars, tinkers and raggle taggle gypsies who were at the bottom of the social ladder and whose future could only lie in the workhouse.

Some few rungs up, and sub-divided, came the working classes. At its lower end were the unskilled labourers and the unemployed. A few rungs higher was the "respectable working class" of skilled workers, mechanics, engineers, drivers of trains, trams and buses, tradesmen and shop assistants, and at the top were the lower ranks of the Civil Service, the white collar workers, bank clerks and clerical assistants. We were conscious that somewhere higher up was a middle class of bankers, lawyers and the medical and military professions, but their ways of life were remote from ours. The working classes rarely had the need, the knowledge or the money to use their services. We were vaguely aware that way up the ladder was something called the aristocracy; a charmed circle of dukes and duchesses, lords and ladies, euphemistically referred to as "one's betters" and whose lives were as far removed from ours as those of fairytale characters. Topping the scale we all knew of a benevolent monarchy; its activities deferentially reported by a press that avoided any references to scandalous behaviour.

Within these grades were further measures of "respectability" depending on the furniture we possessed, the clothes we wore, the way we spoke and the road we lived in (even the particular end of the road in some cases). Friends and relations were taken into account. Anyone whose mother had been a lady's maid, who had an aunt who was "in service" or an uncle who was a bank clerk was assured of a rise of at least one rung in the social scale. Conversely, anyone who had come into conflict with the law sank to the bottom with little hope of recovery.

There were some good-natured grumbles among the inhabitants over being landed in such an inhospitable and inaccessible spot. The only communication with the rest of the city was by an infrequent Midland "Red"

7

bus service that plied between Sutton Coldfield and Birmingham skirting the estate along College Road. So uncharted was the estate that there was some doubt over what it was to be called and we were left wondering whether our address was Witton Lodge or Perry Common. Eventually Perry Common, Erdington was decided upon which, at least, gave some indication of its location.

We were scarcely organised in our new home when a crop of tousled greying hair appeared over the neighbouring fence. "Are you there Mrs . . . er . . . um . . .?" called its owner, florid-faced and with a cascade of chins that rippled down towards a full bosom. Beneath her grizzled, unkempt mop a pair of bright, beady eyes and a broad smile bespoke a big-heartedness. Coming from the kitchen, my mother rectified the impersonal summons by mutual introduction and Mrs Murgatroyd beamed over the fence and offered a steaming cup of tea. It was the prelude to thirteen years of a neighbourliness that was always friendly but never became intimate; a relationship where privacy behind the dividing privet hedge was respected but where help was always available. Mrs Murgatroyd fed our dog if we were away and my mother cut up her old dresses and made "new" ones for Mrs Murgatroyd's poorly-clad children.

The association could not have been otherwise with one whose existence appeared to be as haphazard and disorganised as ours was regulated and organised, but the mid-day cup of tea and a five-minute exchange of news developed into a ritual. The life of the family next door seemed to be one of placid acceptance of the battle to subsist with five children on the wages of a carpenter. They rarely went anywhere except for an occasional Saturday evening expedition to explore the delights of any public houses within walking distance. Although strongly disapproving of such establishments, my mother tacitly accepted these excursions as the only pleasures in a monotonously dreary life.

It was the habits and colourful language of our like-able dishevelled neighbour that intrigued and added to a vocabulary of the local dialect; rich with colloquial phrases and sometimes so histrionic as to be almost operatic and equally unintelligible. She put rubbish in the "miskin" (dustbin), poured her dishwater down the "suff" (drain) and gave her family "bread and scrape" (lard) for tea. She frequently interrupted conversations with "Yer what?," which could be interpreted as "I beg your pardon," "I don't understand" or simply as an expression of disbelief.

Completely defeated one day by hearing her call after one of her offspring "I'll 'it yer tercher" I asked my mother what a tercher was. She looked nonplussed and then, giving a wry smile, said she thought it must have meant "I'll hit you to hurt you," but she did not wish to hear it repeated. Despite the warning it became a byword in our vocabulary, which expanded daily with Mrs Murgatroyd's command of the vernacular.

Unlike most of the local housewives, who had regular shopping days, Mrs Murgatroyd shopped on a daily basis. She knew to a teaspoon that she would be out of sugar by Thursday but it never seemed to occur to her to buy any until she was. She emerged each morning when she had finished her "moilin' an' toilin'," as she described her housework, to "traipse down the shops" where she spent time "'ummin' an' ahrin'" over what to buy and "inchin' an' pinchin'" to save a few coppers. Each afternoon, when most womenfolk were sewing, mending or entertaining friends to tea she appeared, aproned, arms akimbo, on her front doorstep scanning the landscape. She would claim to be looking for one of her children who ought to have come home from school but had probably "blowed off down the shops instead." "I'm looking for our Raymon" she volunteered. "In case 'e rips his gansey" (jersey). Just what she thought she could do to prevent such an occurrence when our Raymon' was not in sight was a matter for speculation, but no matter, it was a good enough excuse for standing there in anticipation of someone appearing with whom she could pass the time of day. She did not usually have to wait long. The road lay on the way to the bus stop and the shops. The sight of anyone turning the corner was a signal to descend from her vantage point and lean over her front gate from where it was easier to entrap passers by and engage them in exchanges of news and gossip which she could retail, suitably embroidered, to the next wayfarer. She was not a malicious talker and many benefited from her information that someone was ill or needed help.

It was not only on local news that she was well acquainted, but on national as well which she gleaned from those who possessed a wireless set, a rarity until the 1930s. This she disclosed with a dramatic intensity

that you could almost believe she was in frequent communication with Westminster, as her news was usually
ahead of the evening papers. She spoke to all children
with equal warmth, unless she caught them swinging on
her front gate. "The King's very bad" (meaning ill not
wicked), she recounted one day as I passed her gate. "He
caught a chill at the Armistice service. It's just come
through from the Palace," she imparted as one privileged
to enjoy the confidence of royalty.

We looked forward with amused anticipation to her
daily bulletins dispensed as we passed homeward from
school. Would it be Princess Marina's hats ("I think she
must make them herself"), the reporting of the minor
tragedy of having trapped her fingers in the mangle, or
the more serious one of Mrs Farmer's well-being. "She
fell down the stairs. They carted her off in a nambu-
lance," she had recounted a few days earlier with some
degree of relish. "They say the 'all was swimmin' in
blood. Like a butcher's shop it was." Mrs Murgatroyd's
pre-eminence in the gathering and dispensing of information gave her a running start over all others

Few of us had a wireless set before the 1930s, some
families went without a daily paper, and, with the
nearest public library some two miles away in Erdington, people in the streets provided the news and social
intercourse that were the essence of life. The streets were
the backcloth for the real life soap operas but they did
not reveal the dramas enacted in the back gardens. These
were reserved for Mrs Lamoney, sharp featured and
sharper with eyes, whose observations from her kitchen
window supplemented that of Mrs Murgatroyd from her

front gate. Calculation of the positions of wireless aerials disclosed to her just which households had invested in a receiving set (the status symbol of the 1930s). Careful detection of the frequency with which neighbours' curtains were washed or changed was a barometer by which she gauged their industry or indolence, and her scrutiny of the washing lines within view gave her an insight into the habits of the wearers of their contents. "Mrs Hopkins's line broke last Monday. She said all her whites was dragged in the mud. Well, I'm glad she told me they was white for I'd never have known. I swear they never saw the bluebag," she called over the fence one day more in mischief than malice. "I don't know if she ever does any work. She *reads*," Mrs Lamoney continued implying that she regarded reading in the same vein as taking opium. "Reading when her washing was lying on the ground."

But it was the nefarious behaviour of the baker at a house further along the road that intrigued her most and the fact that it was never satisfactorily explained vexed her. "The horse stops outside the house every day. He gives him his oats and then he goes inside and he's in there over an hour. She *says* she gives him his dinner, but why does she always send the little lad out to play while he's there? That's what I'd like to know. In my opinion . . ." she continued, implying that it was not only the horse that needed his oats, but we were much too young to appreciate the significance of her remarks.

Mrs Lamoney made it her business to concern herself with everyone else's if they were foolish enough to disclose it. Her burning curiosity and persistence left any other busybodies at the starting gate, but, to her credit, she was moved by the sight of poorly-clad children wearing torn and unpatched clothing. "Well-patched trousers is the sign of a caring mother," she remarked vaingloriously as if to draw attention to her own efforts in that direction. She reported arrivals and departures at various houses with the precision of a railway timetable. Only Mrs Tebbs defeated her. "No-one ever goes there. She hardly ever speaks. You can't get anything out of her. I suppose it's because she's a Londoner and every-one knows they're peculiar," she remarked. "She talks 'funny' and don't let her children play in the road. I suppose she thinks they might get corrupted."

It was such women as these that dominated our childhood scene. They were around all day and revealed their characters. In the absence of any gossip in front of us in our own home, eavesdropping on conversations became a fascinating pastime. It was not a regrettable occupation. It was natural curiosity and how we learnt what went on in the world around us and of people's thoughts and the problems that beset them. There were few menfolk were around in the daytime. They were shadowy characters, almost fearsome for most children; ogres with whom they were threatened. "Just wait till your father gets home."

We only saw the men rushing past in the early morn-ing to catch a bus or tram or cycling silently by to work. Any neighbouring children playing in gardens were despatched homeward long before the head of the household was expected back home so that his slippers could be placed in the hearth to warm, the fire stoked up and a meal on the table by the time he had removed his coat and boots. Devotion to the breadwinner was implicit. He brought home his wages, his wife cooked and cleaned the home and looked after the children. He dug the garden and she did the shopping. No man with any self-respect would have been seen shopping or carrying a shopping bag, nor would his wife have expected him to. Most men had to work on Saturday mornings and disappeared to the football match in the afternoon, and no-one would ever disturb a man's slumbers on a Sunday afternoon. Few of the men spoke to children playing in the road except to chastise for impeding their progress. They remained remote, un-fathomed and feared, and it was only by noticing which houses they entered that it was possible to determine who someone's father was.

The last of the new tenants arrived in the late summer of 1926. We had few amenities. A grocer's, the College Stores, was the only shop. There was nowhere people could meet, no church, pub, bank or library, and we were too far from Erdington for tradesmen to deliver. No-one owned a car and few had bicycles. None possessed a telephone. It would have been of little use if they had. Who would they telephone? Few, except business people knew how to use one.

Lack of established structures for social intercourse meant that new ones had to be devised and it was not long before these were being welded over garden fences; children often supplying the flux. My brother and I were, as yet, too young to be allowed beyond the garden gate, where we would stand envying the children who passed by with jam jars of fiddlers and jackbannocks they had caught in the little brook. Older children sometimes went by clutching a few coppers earned by helping the local farmers with haymaking.

Communications improved when the Number 1 tram route was extended as Route Number 78 from Stockland Green to a new terminus at the bottom of Perry Common Road. The half-mile walk from the top end of the estate to the terminus was justified by a fare that was one penny cheaper than that of the Midland "Red" bus, but it was not until the Number 5 bus route that ran to town via Witton was inaugurated that a satisfactory service was provided. The terminus was at the top of Perry Common Road and the fare to town was fourpence (less than 2p).

Punctuality of the service was assured by the Bundy clock at the terminus where the drivers had to "clock in" their departure times. A late departure because of fog or snow could sometimes be excused, but woe betide any driver who left early. He put his job in jeopardy. The buses were from a new batch of AEC top-covered ones that became standard in the city for many years. They were a big improvement on the open-topped ones that ran on the few bus routes that supplemented the vast network of tramways. The new buses ran on pneumatic tyres and their upholstered seats gave passengers a more comfortable ride. The drivers were not so fortunate. Their only protection from the weather was a tarpaulin that could be drawn up from the engine bulkhead and secured to the underside of the projecting canopy. It left the driver's face exposed to driving rain, sleet, snow and

15

choking winter fogs. The manual gear change on these early petrol-driven buses was hard work.

The conductors fared little better. They had to stand on an open platform at the back of the vehicle, but Mr Sanders, who drove one of the buses, said that the crews liked the new vehicles, except in severe weather when their gloves sometimes froze to the steering wheel. Drivers of the single-deck Midland "Red" buses were more fortunate. They had enclosed half cabs and the conductors were able to shelter inside the saloon where the seats exuded the pungent aroma of real leather, a luxury denied to travellers on corporation vehicles, but the letters SOS that appeared on the wheel hub caps and radiators were, in our youthful imagination, a disincentive to travel on the red buses. The letters seemed to foreshadow imminent disaster.

Progress with motor buses had been rapid since the end of the war but had not yet reached the stage of complete reliability. The buses had difficulty on steep hills, sometimes overheating and breaking down completely, and, unless the passengers could be accommodated on the next, they had a choice of sitting in an unheated vehicle to await the arrival of a relief or walking. The trams were much more reliable. They never broke down.

There were further improvements to the estate when a block of half a dozen shops opened on the South side of the Circle. In the absence of any meeting place the new shops became a popular rendezvous, especially now that the bus terminus had been moved there. The womenfolk gathered there to do their shopping and exchange news and gossip. The children sent on errands after school lingered there and the menfolk as they jumped off the buses on their way home from work called to buy their tobacco and cigarettes. Few of us had a wireless set and not everyone could afford a newspaper so the news gathered during these encounters was retold at home, punctuated with "I heard it down at the shops," which seemed to guarantee authenticity.

The windows of Mr and Mrs Hunt's grocery shop at the corner of Wendover Road were so crammed with dummy packets and pyramids of tinned goods that it was impossible to see inside. Next door was a greengrocer whose produce spilled onto the pavement displayed in wooden crates mounted on swathes of imitation grass. Nearby was the newsagents, tobacconist, sweets and toys, in which was incorporated the Post Office and run by Mr and Mrs Dudley. It was a shop where we spent a great deal of time, noses flattened against the window, contemplating how to spend our few coppers of pocket money. The window not devoted to stationery and magazines was filled with the most exciting things; bags of marbles and "glarncys" (large coloured ones), liquorice sticks, "gob stoppers", "kali suckers" mixed in with an assortment of whips and tops, skipping ropes, and bags of "five stones". There were regiments of lead soldiers, farm animals and lithographed tin replicas of vehicles, all of which had revolving wheels and cost only one penny. Mr Dudley also sold Hornby train set accessories and Meccano parts, but these were too expensive for pocket money and could only be bought with birthday money. Inside the shop and clipped onto a wire that held an assortment of twopenny magazines was

17

a selection of penny models printed on sheets of thin card from which the parts had to be cut and assembled with glue which took ages to set, but the models gave me hours of pleasure.

A butcher's and a fish and chip shop stood next to that of the chemist. In his windows bottles of cough mixture, syrup of figs, brimstone and treacle, jars of "Virol" and packets of "Snowfire" and "Vick" were crowded onto glass shelves. High above these medicaments stood two enormous glass bottles shaped like decanters and filled with coloured liquids; one green the other blue. They were the symbols of the chemist's profession and their contents were the subject of much speculation.

Inside the shop the atmosphere contrasted sharply with the levity that prevailed in the others. There was an air of religious solemnity and people spoke in hushed tones as they waited for the chemist to make up prescriptions. Few went into the shop for toilet requisites, films, cosmetics or any of the absolute essentials of today. They were either unknown or too expensive. We were, however, permitted one extravagance; Gibbs dentifrice which claimed to protect our "ivory castles" and an ambulance box containing boracic and basilicon ointments and a selection of bandages. For many, old rags served to cover cuts and abrasions, and everyone tore up the previous week's newspapers into small squares and threaded them onto a piece of string to hang on a nail inside the lavatory door for use as toilet paper.

Anyone seen leaving the chemist's was usually assumed to have someone ill at home. It demanded solicitous enquiries, especially if a neighbour's child was seen emerging. Children were unable to say with any precision what an illness was. Almost invariably the reply was "It's Mom — 'er's bin took." "Then tell her I'll be round to cook your father's dinner," was an almost certain reply. There were no home helps but there was no shortage of offers of help from willing neighbours, and the wellbeing of the breadwinner took precedence over ministering to the sick. His health was paramount and if he fell ill the whole family was put in jeopardy.

Good health could not be taken for granted. Few expected to escape from winter ailments. Severe weather, air pollution, inadequate heating and undernourishment laid large numbers low. Disabilities in children were evident in the number we saw wearing leg irons to straighten legs deformed by rickets, and there were men around in permanent distress from shell shock and the effects of poisoned gas they had sustained during the Great War.

Having provided a bus service and a few shops, the city authorities appeared to have accomplished all they intended. People grumbled because there were no swimming baths and no library, but there were no organised channels through which they could appeal. The Municipal Bank did open a part-time branch in a little wooden hut near to the shops, but this benefited most of the population very little. Our mother and father transferred their accounts there and opened ones for my brother and me to encourage us to bank some of any money given to us.

The foundation stone of Saint Martin's Church, a

daughter church of Aston's Saint Peter and Saint Paul was laid and excavations were begun for the erection of a public house, but when the church was consecrated and the "Crossways" was opened they polarised the population instead of cementing it.

Of greater significance was the opening of the Co-operative Society's 81st branch near to the existing shops. It was destined to play a significant role in the social and political life of a population eager to improve its lot but not equipped with sufficient knowledge to do much to bring it about. The younger housewives were not even entitled to vote at election times.

Mr Owen managed the Co-op butcher's shop. Each morning he sprinkled sawdust onto the floor of his shop. We understood that this was intended to soak up any blood that dripped from the carcasses of meat that were hung around the shop. Mr Lancaster, a war veteran with a pronounced limp, managed the grocery department. He kept his assistants occupied, when they were not attending to customers, making up grocery orders from lists left by his customers. These were deftly packed in strong brown paper and tied with string ready for delivery by the grocery boy who cycled round the estate on his bicycle and earned half-a-crown (12p) a week.

Along the left-hand counter of the shop, and displayed on crock slabs, were mounds of butter, from which slices were taken with two wooden butter pats and slapped into oblong blocks, weighed on a pair of brass scales and wrapped in greaseproof paper. Cheese was similarly displayed but cut, in accordance with customers' requirements, with a wire attached to a wooden handle.

Bacon was sliced on a hand-operated machine. Behind the opposite counter were the dry goods; pyramids of tinned and packeted food, large tins containing loose biscuits that had to be extracted, weighed and wrapped. Inevitably some got broken and were disposed of to children who went into the shop for "a pennyworth of broken biscuits." Sugar, tea and dried fruits were scooped from hessian sacks that stood on the floor and were weighed into little blue bags.

There were few ready-wrapped commodities and the purchase of groceries that had to be cut, weighed and then wrapped took some time, but time didn't seem to matter. There was no urgency and shops were places where people met to talk. Mr Lancaster and his assistants soon got to know their customers. He called us all by our names and invited his customers to take a seat while being attended to. Payment was always in cash and the customer's share number was written in triplicate in a book of perforated receipts. The top copy was detached and, together with the money, was placed in a cylindrical container which the assistant attached to an overhead wire. He pulled a lever that propelled the cylinder along the wire and rang a bell to alert the female cashier, who sat behind a glass screen on a raised dais, of the approaching projectile. The cashier put the change and the receipt back into the cylinder which rocketed back to the counter for the assistant to unscrew and hand change and receipt to the customer.

The third Co-operative shop was the confectioner's, to which my brother and I were despatched on alternate days in quest of the daily bread. We grumbled at the

21

errand but did get to know the young manageress, Rose, who attempted to dispel our gloom with good-humoured banter. It was a feature of the Co-operative Bakery to produce each week a special cake with which to tempt customers. This confection was offered for one shilling (5p), bore an exotic name but was always a sponge. Sometimes it had jam in the middle and cream on top, sometimes there was cream in the middle and jam on top and sometimes the jam was squeezed into three "portholes" that had been punctured in the top layer. On one occasion, to the merriment of the enlightened, the bakery excelled itself by describing the comestible as a "gateau cake". The name was never repeated. Someone with a knowledge of French must have told them.

Tea in Town

There was but one disadvantage in our new life; we were a long way from town, and a return journey that had previously cost fourpence for us on the tram now cost one and eightpence on the bus. "Erdington is town for us," said my father with a wry smile and, until a new bus route, Number 21, began to run from the Common to the top of Station Road, the only way of getting there was by Shanks's pony on a four-mile trek once a fortnight just to change our library books, but this was usually combined with some shopping along the "village" as local people called the long straggling High Street.

Alan and I were not impressed. There was just one toy shop, which was not of the kind that you could go in "just to look" like Lewis's or Barnby's. There was a small market in a corrugated iron structure, an even smaller Woolworth's and the so-called department store of W.M. Taylor; a dreary two-storey concern that had none of the excitement of the stores in town. On our first visit there was one familiar sight; the old crone who sang the *Glory Song* in town stood at the top of Station Road where her toneless drone was extracting a few coppers from the passers-by. Her aspirations that "it will be glory to look on his face" were soon to be realised. She collapsed and died one day shortly afterwards and it was reported that she had over one hundred pound notes sewn into her petticoats.

It was only the promise of an occasional Saturday afternoon bus ride into town that gave my brother and me any consolation. We always travelled on the top deck of the bus so that our father could smoke his pipe, and we could enjoy a bird's eye view of the suburban streets which could not be appreciated from street level. There were shop blinds with the shopkeepers' names printed on them, *Turog* and *Hovis* picked out in gold above a baker's shop and the Maypole and George Mason's, shop signs suspended from lattice brackets and barber's poles heaven-inclined. Enamelled advertisements for Mazawattee Tea and Johnnie Walker Whisky seen at eye level lent colour to the drab buildings and the upper decks of passing tramcars. Examples of the stonemason's and ironmaster's arts were there in profusion. Horse troughs and drinking fountains abounded. There were ornamental clocks suspended over jeweller's shop windows, wrought ironwork adorned the tram standards and the delicate filigree, spires and spikes on some of the public conveniences gave them the appearance of fifteenth century baptistries.

Everyone seemed to be in town on Saturday afternoons. It was the only time most of them could be. The men worked in the mornings and the shops were shut on Sundays. There was excitement and pageantry in the streets vibrating with the noise of vehicles — many still horse-drawn — a growing number of cars, and vans and lorries of inestimable variety from some thirty British manufacturers all making substantial profits without government subsidies.

Buses forged a way through the maelstrom and tram

drivers clanged their gongs incessantly to clear a way through the traffic that impeded their progress along inflexible tracks. "It's time the trams were scrapped," was oft repeated but it was more than twenty years before the last tram left the city's streets. The kerbsides bristled with flower sellers, musicians, hawkers and organ grinders, all adding to the tumult. Some respite from the noise could be sought in the tranquillity of the Great Western Arcade where we spent time, noses glued to the windows of Barnby's famous toyshop, gazing at the display of working mechanical toys we could never hope to possess.

Lewis's also had a toy department, but it was only at Christmastime that they indulged in animated displays. It was here that we saw the real Father Christmas in his grotto. Those in other stores were imposters, so we were told, and the bedraggled, red-coated charlatans that thronged the gutters were the worst type of catch-penny merchants who had no business to be there.

But it was not to spend time gazing at toyshop windows that we were taken to town. Our mother's usual objective was bargain hunting for dress materials in the big city stores. She had her favourites; Grey's more so than Lewis's because "Birmingham's own store" as it advertised itself had been founded by a Birmingham family, and Rackham's she preferred to C & A. The Beehive and Moor Street Warehouse were other favourites, inconveniently situated, but offering competitive prices.

She always went to Batchelor's, an old-established fashion house in High Street, for her coats and hats. All this was before she became enthusiastic over the Co-operative Movement and changed her allegiance. She was not enamoured with Marks and Spencer who had opened a small store in High Street and dismissed them with "They only began on a market and don't sell anything costing more than five shillings so their goods can't have much quality."

Weary with our mother's deliberations over price, quality and value for money, we found some relief in contemplating the various mechanical devices used in the larger stores for cash transactions. Those most up-to-date employed pneumatic tubes. The customer's money and a handwritten bill were pushed into a cylindrical container and inserted through an airtight flap into a tube to be conveyed pneumatically to a cashier in a distant counting house. The system that intrigued most was more visible. Money and bill were placed in one half of a hemispherical container which was screwed to the other half to form a sphere that resembled a cannonball. The shop assistant placed this onto a U-shaped overhead railway along which it progressed by gravity, sometimes through several departments to a cash office in a remote part of the store. After an interval the container, with any change and a receipt, returned via a different gravitational route. There were other intriguing means of cash propulsion, and the space above head level in most shops vibrated with projectiles.

Department stores in the 1920s and 30s were very labour-intensive. Every counter, and each department store had many, had its quota of assistants and seats for customers. Each lift had its attendant. He operated outer and inner iron gates. "Ladies dress materials and fashions, furniture and soft furnishings, gents tailoring," he intoned, like one informing a funeral party that the hearse was at the door, as he propelled his load heavenwards.

A special treat was a descent into Lewis's basement to visit their soda fountain, though why soda and why fountain we could never determine, as there seemed to be neither soda nor fountain in evidence, but delicious ice creams were dispensed from behind a high glass counter. There had to be nothing exotic, like the luscious concoction served in a tall glass and topped with fruit and cream, called a "knickerbocker glory". It was far too expensive and we had to be content with a strawberry and vanilla ice served in a metal bowl.

Our father, impatient with vacillation over colour, texture and designs of dress fabrics, and how much would be needed to match the pattern of the material, would disappear in the direction of Combridge's, Cornish's or Hudson's book shop to while away the time more profitably. Although he was fond of reading, he rarely bought a book. He would have felt it to be a guilty extravagance.

Sometimes he took my brother and me with him on excursions through the city streets. For one with a limited formal education, the knowledge he had accumulated about his adopted city was quite remarkable. He showed us the imperial measurements on one of the walls surrounding Chamberlain Square, Tom Thumb's grave and the base of a Town Hall pillar that had fallen and killed some men working on its construction and

27

used as a gravestone in Saint Philip's Churchyard. This thirst after knowledge and travel became even more apparent years later when I was serving overseas with the Royal Air Force. He longed to travel but never got further than Dublin, yet he glimpsed his untravelled world through my eyes and letters, maps and books on my expeditions in Egypt, the Levant, India and Ceylon during the Second World War.

It was on one of these expeditions that I discovered New Street Station. We always travelled from Snow Hill and I was not aware of another station, but one day he decided to take a short cut to the Bull Ring. We went through an archway under the Queen's Hotel and descended some steps to a crowded footbridge. The air reeked with the smell of hot engine oil, clouds of steam hung beneath a vast glass cavern and down below locomotives hissed and simmered. The station was larger, but much dirtier than that at Snow Hill, but it was more exciting because, being an open station, we were allowed onto the platforms without having to pay for a ticket.

From the rear entrance to the station we climbed the steps and through the Doric arch into the Market Hall, crowded with the curious and the bargain hunters. High up on one wall was a mechanical clock featuring little carved and painted figures who struck bells with little hammers to mark the passage of time. The clock became a casualty during the war that was yet to come and it was not replaced. Below were marble-topped counters where dinners were supplied to the market traders who perched on high stools to eat their meals supplied through clouds of steam from bubbling cauldrons. Outside in the Bull Ring, and overshadowed by the statue of Nelson, was an animated scene of jostling crowds seeking last-minute reductions in the fading daylight.

No-one in our wide circle of friends ever went out for a meal. Such a venture would have been considered not only extravagant but ostentatious. There were, in any case, few places to dine other than in the hotels, which to us were unknown territory. Restaurants closed at the same time as the shops and the pubs served drinks only. Between the wars the teashops were where people met. There was a profusion of them. They were refuges from shopping, chatter shops and trysting places. Lyons had several where waitresses called "nippies" served tea and cakes in surroundings of marble and mirrors which made people with little money feel they had more.

Our parents sometimes indulged themselves with tea in Pattison's, Kunzle's or Boots, where a more sublime atmosphere prevailed; polished wood, frescoed ceilings, white tablecloths, and where a trio played selections of teatime music; Strauss, Lehar and excerpts from Gilbert and Sullivan operas. Orders were taken by a waitress in a black dress, a white apron, and a frilled cap, and recorded on a little pad attached to her waist by a long piece of string. The tea came in pots along with china cups, a bowl of lump sugar, the cakes in little paper jackets. We had to watch our table manners, but felt very grand. We were really living and seeing the world.

The journey home in the deepening gloom of a winter evening had its enchantment. From the top of the bus we were at eye level with the gas street lamps, prisms of glass topped with a metal ventilator and adorned with an outstretched arm to receive the lamp cleaner's ladder and shedding pools of light on the shifting scene below. With undisguised curiosity we permitted ourselves fleeting glances into the living rooms of those who had neglected to draw their curtains.

Woman, Home and Duty

Washday was always on Monday unless it happened to be a Bank Holiday. It spelled misery for the whole family. Washday could not be changed, even in bad weather, anymore than the Almighty could be expected to postpone his rain because of it. Washing had to be done on Mondays; the domestic routine could not, otherwise, proceed in accordance with preordained plans. A wet washday could extend the misery for three days while the washing was dried on a wooden clothes horse around the living room fire, precluding the family from its warmth and filling the room with steam and rank smells.

The ordeal began at seven o'clock in the morning with the lighting of the fire under the bathroom copper to heat the water. Breakfast was a hurried affair and the breakfast crocks had to be cleared away and the beds made in advance of the usual time and before the water in the copper came to the boil. We were glad to escape to school to avoid the ensuing turmoil, which could be worse compounded if the fire refused to burn. This was a frequent occurrence. The firebox was temperamental and the draught critical. Unless the kitchen door was ajar it refused to draw. There was no time to spare and during school holidays we were in the way. Playing in the garden was restricted and impeded by clothes props and billowing sheets hung on the washing line. A broken clothes line was a disaster of the first magnitude and we would be press-ganged into rescuing mud-spattered clothing from the ground so that the whole washing process could be repeated.

While the water was being brought to the boil my father's dirty overalls from the previous week were spread on the terracotta floor, soaked in paraffin and scrubbed to remove the accumulation of oil and grease. The paraffin-soaked articles were then laid on one side to be washed later, first with soda and then with soap to remove the last vestiges of dirt. It was then an employee's responsibility to provide his own protective clothing and have it laundered. It was a matter of pride for every wife to send her husband to work each Monday with overalls

unblemished, well-ironed and meticulously folded.

By this time the water in the copper would be boiling and was drawn off a bucket at a time and carried from bathroom to kitchen to fill the wash tub. At one time this had been a heavy wooden barrel but this was replaced in later years by a lighter galvanised article. The clothes were pushed with a stick into the hot water and soap was added. Detergents, fabric conditioners and biological powders were beyond prediction, and such washing powders as there were, "Rinso" and "Persil", were suspiciously regarded as an unnecessary extravagance. A bar of washing soap was laboriously pared into flakes with a knife and deposited in the tub. Water, melting soap and clothes were then attacked with a "washmaid" or "dolly" as it was sometimes called. This was a heavy wooden block resembling a three-legged stool with a long handle protruding from the top. It was gripped with both hands and plunged up and down to agitate the water and extract the dirt from the clothes. It required considerable energy, and many women could be heard exclaiming at the end of the process that they were "wore out," yet their toil was far from ended.

The tub had to be emptied a bucket at a time because it was far too heavy to lift or tip. It was then refilled with rinsing water. White garments were rinsed yet again. This time in the sink and in water in which a "blue bag" was inserted. This was purported to "whiten" the clothes, but the blueness imparted satisfied any curiously-observant neighbours that acknowledged procedures had been complied with.

The clothes were extracted one by one and fed between the rollers of a mangle that stood in the kitchen corner. Two heavy wooden rollers, supported on a cast iron frame were operated by turning a handle attached to a large wheel. This drove a complicated system of cogwheels and gears that caused the rollers to revolve and extract the remaining water from the dripping clothes that were fed between them. During school holidays we were sometimes asked to turn the mangle. We rarely objected. It gave rein to our inventive imaginations. We became train or tram drivers, but our varying speeds, depending on the stages of the imaginary journey, must have frustrated the most patient of mothers.

As Monday was the washday at all the neighbouring houses gardens were soon bedecked with waving sheets, shirts, towels and pillowslips. Pants, vests and petticoats, except those of Mrs Tebbs, flapped unabashed in familiar proximity over neighbouring fences. Mrs Tebbs, because of the personal nature of such intimate garments or their condition, preferred to dry them indoors. The non-appearance on the clothes line of such "unmentionables" caused some comment among the inquisitive, and the insatiable curiosity of Mrs Lamoney provoked raised eyebrows and her speculation that "It makes you wonder if they wear any!"

The penultimate task on washday was to starch all linen, which comprised tablecloths, sheets, shirt fronts, and the frills and flounces on female apparel. Men's collars were stiff loose ones that were attached to the shirt by two brass studs that left dirty marks on the neck. The collars were sent to the laundry because it was too difficult to stiffen them at home. They were returned so stiffly starched that they cut into the neck, but this had to be stoically borne; it ensured that there was no slouching. The head had to be carried erect, severe soreness around the chin otherwise resulted.

With evening, and provided it had been good drying day, the task of ironing loomed. Two flat metal irons were needed; one to be used while the other was being heated propped up on a trivet against the firebars. As each garment was ironed it was put onto a clothes horse to be aired. Our houses had no airing cupboards and it would have been unthinkable to have put clothes away in drawers until they had been thoroughly aired. So many illnesses were attributed to the putting on of insufficiently-aired clothing.

If all had gone well, washday could be completed by nine o'clock in the evening. It would have taken more than twelve hours of hard work, interrupted only for the preparation of meals, and now it would be time for the supper arrangements to be put in hand.

A good washday left our mothers free to devote the rest of the week to their homes and families which were paramount. Sex equality was not a problem that worried anyone. The sexes were complementary not equal. Fathers were the breadwinners, mothers the home-makers and rearers of children. Our families were units where children remained until they married. An un-married mother would have stood as much chance of obtaining a council house as King Canute did of com-manding the tides. Few women went out to work. They were expected to give up their jobs on marriage and each to make a home for her husband and bring up his children.

A woman going out to work invited censure. Mrs Corris alone in our road went out to work. She was an object of sympathy and blame. "She must be neglecting her home," vouchsafed Mrs Lamoney to Mrs Murga-troyd as she returned from an early expedition to the shops. "It's a pity she has to go out to work, but her husband's only a bricklayer. He can't earn much, but it's not right. She's taking a job off a man." This was extremely unlikely as jobs were not usually inter-changeable, but her comments reflected people's thinking that a woman's place was in the home. Mrs Murgatroyd would have detained her for further delectation, but Mrs Lamoney's remark over neglect of duty pricked her own conscience as she exclaimed with alarm "Just look at the time. I must go. Ten o'clock and not a po emptied!" There was no indoor sanitation in our houses and the emptying and washing of bedroom chamber pots was but one of the essential daily rituals, as was the emptying of the ashes from the previous day's fire and laying paper, firewood and coal for the next one.

To us, as children, our homes seemed to exist not so much for relaxation and enjoyment but as places that had to be constantly swept and dusted, where furniture was interminably polished, rugs were shaken and floors scrubbed or polished. It was all very well while we were at school but, during holidays, these chores reduced life to purgatory. We were forever in the way and thrust into the garden.

Tuesday was bedroom day when all the rugs were shaken out of the window and left hanging out to "freshen" while the linoleum floor covering and furniture were polished. This took most of the morning, interrupted only for the preparation and cooking of the mid-day meal, which was never lunch in Birmingham but dinner. On Wednesdays and Thursdays there was some respite from housework, and our mother devoted these days to shopping, mending, dressmaking, an occasional visit to town or visiting or entertaining friends.

Friday, in readiness for the weekend, was the workday *par excellence* whether visitors were expected or not. The downstairs rooms were in turmoil. The living room rugs were thrown into the garden where they were hung on a line and beaten to remove the dust. The linoleum was polished on hands and knees. Wall-to-wall carpeting was inconceivable. It could not be turned to prevent excessive wear, neither could it be satisfactorily cleaned because vacuum cleaners were rare possessions. Linoleum was best. It was hard wearing, it could be cleaned properly, and, with a hearthrug, provided all the decoration and warmth considered necessary.

A vigorous attack on the furniture with polish and what was termed "elbow grease" and the black leading of the firegrate ensued before the living room was returned to its earlier condition and attention could be directed to the kitchen and bathroom, which were so ill-equipped that only the gas stove, sink and bath needed attention. The main effort was to scrub the tiled floors and cover them with newspapers to prevent recoiling until these were removed on Saturday afternoons. My mother permitted herself one extravagance; that of a window cleaner who trundled his ladder and bucket round the estate roads on a two-wheeled truck. One of the few sitting-down tasks was that of polishing the "silver". There was no stainless steel and all cutlery had to be polished regularly to prevent tarnishing.

Girls were expected to help with the housework but not so the boys, which was to their disadvantage when, a few years later, they were conscripted into the armed forces not knowing how to thread a needle or darn a pair of socks. Washing up the breakfast crocks and peeling the vegetables on Sunday mornings were the only chores my brother and I were expected to do. Why this situation existed is difficult to imagine. Presumably it was because as long as the menfolk brought in the money the womenfolk were expected to provide a comfortable home and bring up their children. On Friday evenings the men brought home their pay packets. My father's remained unopened until he arrived home, when he gave our mother the housekeeping allowance and kept the rest for himself and for giving us treats. In some cases the man gave his wife the pay packet from which she took what she required and handed the man his pocket money.

There was an eye-opener for us one Friday evening as we were passing Kynoch's factory gates just as the men were coming out and we saw from the top deck of the bus a clutch of women waiting for their menfolk to appear. It was not out of fondness for their spouses, we were told, but to ensure that they got hold of their money before their menfolk disappeared into the *Witton Arms* to indulge themselves before returning home the worse for drink and with a depleted pay packet. Such alarming behaviour was foreign to us; a Victorian hangover that lingered long in childhood memory and of a time when women were entirely dependent on a man's wages to provide for their families.

Friday night was also bath night and, like wash day, was a fixed feast in the calendar. The cost of an extra fire to heat the bath water and the effort expended precluded more than one bath per week. As on washday the bath water had to be heated in the copper and drawn off by the bucketful to fill the cast iron bath. A vigorous application of carbolic soap was the prelude to a brisk rubbing and hair wash. The bathroom floor was of terracotta tiles and cold to the feet, but when we got out of the bath the copper door was thrown open so that we could dry ourselves in the warm glow of the fire while the copper was being refilled for our parents' bath later.

The Seller of Salt, Doctors and Sudden Death

About four times a year, although there was no guarantee of this, a withered crone known to us only as the salt woman trundled the estate roads pushing a three-wheeled basket carriage containing blocks of salt protected by layers of sacking. Her approach, heralded by protracted cries of "Salt," could be heard in the next road and even beyond in the still air of a summer's day. To anyone unfamiliar with her cry it must have sounded like the agonised wail of a combatant animal in its death throes, but it was joyfully received by the housewives to whom refrigerators and deep freezers were unknown and who used salt for preserving.

The salt woman was a lugubrious and time-worn creature clad always in the same sad relics of clothing: a voluminous ankle-length skirt of dark worsted fabric and a shabby grey shawl pulled tightly around her throat and fastened with a large safety pin. Her sparse grey hair was drawn back from her weatherworn features and secured, not as might have been expected by a man's cloth cap, but beneath the sagging brim of a shapeless black hat of shiny material. A large hatpin secured her millinery fast against sudden levitation by a gust of wind. She would bring her carriage to a halt halfway along the road and throwing off the sacking, reveal her commodity to those who had gathered in response to her rallying cry. With a vicious-looking knife she carved her blocks of salt in accordance with the instructions of those assembled. Her transactions completed and any enquiries concerning her next visit disposed of with a melancholy "Depends 'ow long I'm spared" she recovered her burden and, renewing her anguished wail, shuffled along into the next road.

There were other frequenters; the chimney sweep who carried his brushes over his shoulder and a knife and scissors grinder who arrived on a bicycle which he propped up alongside the kerb and used as a mechanical drive for his grindstone. Tinkers materialised offering to mend leaking kettles and saucepans with washers and rivets.

The corncure man, whose shabby blue serge suit seemed at variance with his well-modulated voice, occasionally appeared. His medical knowledge, genuine or assumed, impressed those whose feet were troublesome. On each doorstep he produced from a small attaché case, which he propped against the doorpost, an assortment of medicaments in little coloured bottles, cutting implements and a selection of pads to relieve the pain of corns and bunions. His soft-spoken voice and knowledgeable posture impressed even those who were not afflicted and sometimes tempted them to buy from one whose demeanour suggested that he was of gentler birth than most others who knocked on doors. He came for many years but remained an enigma. There were also gypsies and pedlars hawking pegs, lace and other small household items from baskets they carried from door to door.

The rag and bone man came more often, clad in badly-fitting, ill-matched clothing and a torn cap that may well have been taken from his load. He traipsed the estate roads alongside an open two-wheeled cart pulled by a horse that was in the last stages of decrepitude. A low-pitched, drawn-out blast on a dented tin horn followed by a mournful cry of "Raggerbone!" signalled his approach. His trumpet call sent all children within earshot scampering off to scrounge any old trousers, jackets, curtains and the like, and which were of no further use, in the hope that the rag and bone man would, in exchange, surrender a goldfish that was most likely to be half dead from the effects of being sloshed around in a galvanised bath on the back of his cart.

I never discovered why the man wanted bones, nor did I ever see any offered. In such an eventuality I imagine they would have been ground down for use as fertilisers, but I never knew. Contact with the rag and bone man was not encouraged, and any dealings with him were transacted at a distance from his cart, which was not only deemed to be flea-ridden but also contaminated with the causative agents of diseases, referred to collectively as "the fever" of which there was an ever-present dread. The nature and names of all but the most common ailments were little understood, either through ignorance or because there was so little rapport between patients and the doctor, of whom most were in awe.

Doctors were several notches above the working classes in the social scale and it was unimaginable that the two should meet other than professionally. It would have been acutely embarrassing to both. As a result there was a reluctance by patients and their relatives to question doctors, most of whom seemed disinclined to discuss pathological conditions in terms which their patients could understand. Misunderstandings and anxieties were inevitable.

There was no National Health Service and doctors expected to be paid at the time they gave their services. A visit to the surgery cost half-a-crown (12p) and was only undertaken when attempts at home treatment had failed. A foreboding atmosphere of impending doom pervaded the bleak and gloomy waiting room to which I was sometimes despatched reluctantly on an errand of mercy to collect a bottle of medicine for a sick neighbour. A few wisps of smoke rose from the ashes in the fireplace and did little to warm or cheer the patients who sat in a silence punctuated only by coughs, groans and sneezes, stifled so that they would not fail to hear the "ping" of the little brass bell that the doctor rang to summon the next patient. He had no receptionists or secretaries and kept his own records in a cabinet near to his desk and did his own dispensing, managing without the assistance of health visitors, dieticians, physiotherapists or social workers to follow up cases. The district nurse, who rode around the estate in a distinctive uniform on a bicycle, carrying her little black bag, was all the help he had.

A home visit by the doctor cost the equivalent of 25p and, as few were in a position to budget for illnesses the doctor was only sent for in extreme cases, and often not until a patient was beyond his help.

The "wonder drugs" lay many years ahead and for anyone contracting influenza, diphtheria or tuberculosis, recovery could not be guaranteed. The catching of any kind of "fever" was a cause for alarm and apprehension with an ever-present threat of death. Rumours and super-stitions over the sources from which anyone could catch the "fever" abounded. In addition to dealing with the rag and bone man we were discouraged from putting coins in the mouth, sucking keys or privet leaves, picking up discarded cigarette cards and tram tickets from the gutter or inhaling from "smelly" drains. The real causes of most illnesses were, in all probability, bad working con-ditions, air pollution and lack of warmth and adequate clothing.

The approach of winter was dreaded because of the choking fogs, aggravated by the smoke from thousands of domestic and factory chimneys, that engulfed the city each winter. Visibility, reduced to a few feet, brought traffic to a standstill. Only the trams on their fixed tracks pushed on through the gloom which the street lamps failed to penetrate, their drivers incessantly clanging their gongs. In their wakes along the tramlines came crocodiles of shadowy figures who saw no sense in parting with a tram fare to be carried no faster than they could walk. If we had to go out it was with nose and mouth protected by a handkerchief. Crossing any road was an adventure. The density of the fog obscured all reference points and people lost a sense of direction.

At such times bronchitis was especially feared

because it was often the precursor of pneumonia. Steaming kettles were introduced into the sickroom to ease the patient's breathing and, apart from prescribing an expectorant, seemed to be all that a doctor could recommend. The onset of double pneumonia was an almost certain death knell. The doctor would apprise the family of the expected time of the "crisis" and the sudden change for better or worse was awaited with resignation. A piece of cloth was tied round the door knocker to deaden its sound, voices were lowered and household tasks carried out listlessly in an atmosphere of impending doom. Influenza was similarly dreaded. Memories of the toll exacted during the immediate post-war epidemic were too close for complacency and any muscular aches or a sore throat were viewed with concern lest they be the forerunners of the infection.

Stringent precautions were taken to reduce the spread of any infection. A dampened sheet was hung across a sickroom door, vessels used during attendance were scalded and any library books on the premises had, by regulation, to be removed and disinfected before being returned to circulation.

To try to avoid the crippling costs of medical treatment, those who could afford them tried elementary home cures and took precautions. We were dosed daily with "Virol" to keep healthy. Coughs were treated with spoonsful of brimstone and treacle. Cod liver oil was horrible to take but was deemed to be essential during the winter months. California syrup of figs kept the bowels healthy and a mixture of vinegar and water was considered to be an antidote for sore throats. The spring was also considered to be a "dangerous time" when sulphur was forced down our throats to keep them free from infection. Yeast, bought by the pennyworth from the chemist, tasted horrible but was administered to keep the complexion healthy and prevent spots. Except for smallpox there was no vaccination against the many infectious and contagious diseases that were prevalent, and everyone expected to catch measles, mumps and whooping cough. There were many "killer diseases" and, without antibiotics, illnesses lasted longer and often left victims with life-long complications.

The appearance in the road of the doctor's car caused excitement and concern. Excitement because it was the only car likely to be seen there and concern because someone was so ill that the doctor had had to be sent for. The afflicted household was kept under surveillance from behind the curtains of nearby homes and, as soon as the doctor had departed, the anxious neighbours popped across. Help was never far away in such a close-knit community and there were plenty of offers to run to the chemist or look after children.

Removal to hospital was viewed with the gravest concern, especially by the older generation who regarded hospitals as places to which the seriously ill were removed as a last resort and from which they were rarely expected to return. This was, of course, quite untrue, but was an outlook coloured by fearful tales and recollections of their own youth.

The arrival of an ambulance, before such vehicles were common sights used for transporting patients for physiotherapy or case follow-up, aroused a mixture of curiosity and sympathy. Neighbours gathered by custom to await the emergence of the stretcher-borne patient wrapped in a red blanket. "Why is it a red one?" I asked a curious Mrs Murgatroyd as one of our neighbours, Mr Letting, was borne by on a stretcher. "It's so's the blood won't show," I just had time to hear before being snatched indoors by my mother. "You can watch weddings and share people's happiness but don't ever stand and gloat over people in distress," she said. I watched from the window to see people mouthing a few words of comfort and sympathy before the ambulance doors clanged to leaving a bereft and bewildered family. None had cars or telephones to maintain contact, and there were long periods without news that could only be passed in contemplation, speculation, hope and prayer. Hospital discipline was strict and visiting severely restricted.

Communication from the hospital could only be made by a policeman, whose appearance on the doorstep was dreaded. He was never the bearer of good news, only of worsening or bad for those whose worries were intensified by apprehension over where the money for the next week's food was to come from if the victim happened to be the breadwinner. All that a family could expect would be fifteen shillings (75p) from a health scheme not directly administered by the government but by approved societies to which employees could make voluntary contributions. If they neglected to do so there was nothing but to rely on relatives or appeal to the Public Assistance Committee.

The approved societies also paid a capitation fee to a

doctor so that the insured person became a panel patient as opposed to a fee-paying one. Hospital patients were charged according to their means by the voluntary hospitals and those run by local authorities since 1929. Some of the costs could be defrayed by employees who were contributors to the Birmingham Hospital Saturday Fund which had resulted from an appeal some years earlier to the working classes for funds to improve hospital conditions. Those who agreed to a reduction of one penny a week from their wages received some compensation upon admission to hospital.

It was a peculiarity of the era that anyone who was "on the panel" but not actually ill in bed was generally considered by their less charitable neighbours to be fit enough to work. As a result there were many men who, rather than be thought malingerers, returned to work before they were sufficiently recovered, sometimes with tragic results.

A period of convalescence was allowed for those recovering from serious illnesses and some altruistic firms provided convalescent homes where they sent recovering employees for one or two weeks before they returned to work. A man convalescing at home was subjected to rigorous supervision by sick visitors. He had to be indoors by nine o'clock in the evening. If he were found not to be, and in the absence of a very good excuse, he lost his benefit. There was a long way to go before the financial anxieties of illness were removed by an all-embracing health service.

The sharpness of death cut suddenly into our lives one tragic Whit Monday when an urgent knocking at the front door disturbed our teatime and sent our mother hastily to answer the insistent rapping at the front door. We overheard one of the Bargis's, the school caretaker's boys, imploring mother to come at once. "It's Dad, but Mom says you'll know what to do," he urged as mother responded by dashing across the road with him. The few minutes before she returned gave Mrs Murgatroyd time to emerge to determine the cause of the disturbance, and through the window we saw our mother mouthing "He's gone," before rushing back into the house for two pennies to put on his eyelids.

For the first time we were abruptly brought into close contact with death and, although it did not affect us directly, we played with the Bargis children and the insecurity of life came as a shock. In those days people did not die. The very bluntness of the word numbed. People were said to have passed on, gone to glory or the bosom of Abraham.

The family of anyone who died before World War Two had to endure distressing customs and procedures that had been carried over from the previous century, and were expected by society. Without risking censure they were inescapable. Harrowing as it was, people expected to retain the remains of the deceased in the shelter of the family until the funeral. Removal to a mortuary was only undertaken following the necessity of an inquest. The afflicted family had to suffer agonies from the morbid gapers who came ostensibly to condole but expected to be invited to view the corpse. Their condolences were often supplemented by vivid accounts of their own experiences, punctuated by less than cheerful references to premonitions; the "Death Rattle", the "Death Grip" and other ominous portents they had received from the "Grim Reaper" as forewarnings. Assurances that it was God's will brought little comfort, however well-intentioned.

There was much to be done and without the aid of telephones and cars. Relatives had to be informed, funeral arrangements made and, after the interment, the erection of a suitable memorial and the printing of black-bordered memorial cards had to be contemplated.

However poor a family was somehow the money was found to provide a funeral commensurate with society's requirements. Some people contributed to a penny a week burial fund, others were in insurance schemes, but these rarely covered the expenses incurred, and under-takers, tailors, florists and monumental masons flourished on bereavements. Mourners attended funerals in black attire, the women were often veiled and some wore mourning jewellery (Whitby jet) handed down by previous generations. For the men a black bowler hat was obligatory, and bespoke tailors prospered by supplying mourning orders within a few days. Flowers were the only acceptable tributes, and orders for wreaths conveying impressions of vacant chairs, harps and heaven's gates were called for from florists.

The demise of a relative however distant imposed obligations. There were occasions following the death of a relative we hardly knew or had never seen when our mother felt obliged to sew a black crepe band around the left arm of our blazers as an outward sign of mourning.

We hated it. It led to embarrassment at school but it had to be borne with fortitude in the interest of decency.

On the day of Mr Bargis's funeral the curtains of all houses in the vicinity had been drawn since early morning and neighbours and friends gathered in silence to pay their last respects. As playmates of the children suddenly bereft of a father we were allowed to stand at the front gate to watch the funeral procession. Motor vehicles were becoming more common in the streets but tradition still demanded a horse-drawn cortege of curious carriages of the kind that had long disappeared from the streets except for their association with funerals. A hush fell over the assembled crowd as the clip-clop of horses hooves signalled the approach of the archaic four-wheeled carriages drawn by black horses, black plumed and driven by top-hatted, crepe-streamered coachmen. Members of the sorrowing family emerged, mounted the vehicles and, preceded by a glass hearse, the melancholy cavalcade disappeared towards Witton Cemetery. The silent crowd dispersed to re-open the curtains.

Only the morbid remained to indulge in reminiscences and speculations. "Little Mrs Perks", a timorous, pale-faced melancholy woman who lived a short distance away, burst into tears she seemed unable to control. She was suffering from a nervous breakdown, for which in the absence of anti-depressant tablets there was no palliative. Sympathy did little to alleviate her suffering and the less sympathetic who urged her to "snap out of it" only aggravated her condition. Her affliction manifested itself in an irrepressible dread of funerals that

51

approached hysteria, yet she was drawn to them like iron filings to a magnet. It was almost as though these distressing events acted as some kind of therapy for her.

A short distance away was the improbable-sounding "auntie" Watkins. Just why she was "Auntie" and not "Mrs" was never clearly established, but the sobriquet stuck and spread.

Auntie Watkins was over-burdened with a tiresome mother who was unable or unwilling to put a foot over the threshold, declared that she could not be left alone and, on the slightest provocation, took to her bed in a fit of pique to await the arrival of "Death's Bright Angel." She confined herself to her armchair or her bed so just why she could not be left was never substantiated. She was hardly likely to fall or set the house ablaze.

It was arguable which of the two was the more capricious; the mother who turned a deaf ear to Gabriel's trumpet or Auntie Watkins who insisted that her mother put on her gloves before receiving visitors at her bedside. It was solicitude for Auntie Watkins that persuaded well-intentioned neighbours to sit with mother while Auntie Watkins did her shopping. According to leaked reports mother was a tyrant and her conversation limited to the frequent warnings she received from angels of death, the recurrent appearances of heavenly hosts, vistas of pearly gates and her proximity to death's door. Mrs Medding, who had a lively, if sometimes wicked, sense of humour that we were quick to appreciate, wondered why no-one had opened the door to satisfy her aspirations. "The old tyrant's a perfect scream," she said in the parlance of the era. On this occasion she happened to be passing by to return a rotten apple she had found among those sold to her by "that greengrocer" who had had the nerve to display a notice "Buy your apples here. Why go elsewhere to be swindled?" If the greengrocer did not appreciate the irony of his announcement, then Mrs Medding was about to make sure that he did.

Mrs Lamoney, who had so far observed the obsequies as custom required suddenly shattered an awkward silence by squawking "Oh look, here's Gladys." Those remaining obeyed her behest as Gladys, flighty daughter of a frivolous mother, swept into view clad in a fur coat that gaped open to reveal a low-cut, semi-transparent blouse and sporting a saucy little hat that partly shaded one eye.

To us as children Gladys was a vision of loveliness, but Mrs Lamoney did not see her that way. "She'll come to a bad end, that girl. There's enough powder on her face to whitewash the kitchen," she twittered with sanctimonious glee. "I wonder where she's off to? I suppose it's her half day off," she speculated. "Good afternoon, Gladys," she volunteered with cold contempt as Gladys flounced by acknowledging her greeting with a saucy smile. "Now how did she come by that fur coat?" Mrs Lamoney persisted, addressing no-one in particular but hoping someone might supply her with an answer. "She's only a shop assistant at Lewis's. Fur coats don't come from the wages of shop girls." But, as it was an open secret that Gladys's mother never saved any money, spent every penny as it came in and boasted that she had nothing in the bank, it was possible that she had bestowed some of her wealth on Gladys's fur coat. Mrs

Lamoney did not think so, and with "It'll be the work-house for her. A painted Jezebel — that's what she is," she disposed of Gladys who was hastening her footsteps towards an approaching bus.

She renewed her vilification of Gladys with allusions to a whited sepulchre until the road was deserted and then, darting her eyes in either direction like a dog look-ing for a lamp post, she turned in at our front gate with the simple request to our mother for some trouser buttons she had been unable to purchase the previous day. She had forgotten it was early closing day. By the time she had rummaged through the button box, punc-tuated by an account of her abortive search for buttons the day before, the funeral cortege had returned for a post-funeral meal, and she was moved by her more charitable nature to express some concern for the widow and her five children. They would be sure to turn her out of her house. They did, but a considerate council re-housed the family, and a new school caretaker arrived to take over.

Mrs Bargis was one of several widows who had been bereft of their husbands to struggle on a meagre pension. Mrs Stormont was one, and Mrs Godfrey's tragedy was compounded by the loss of her only son, for whom she had toiled to send to the Grammar School, when he was shot down a few years later over Germany. Some, Mrs Phillips and Mrs Garner, eventually found work as part-time cleaners at the new library and the *Mayfair* cinema. Others trudged further afield to supplement their widows' pensions of ten shillings (50p) a week.

Life then was very insecure and, with social security

many years away, there was always anxiety over illnesses and the possibility of accidents that could drastically change a way of life. A drenching at an exposed bus stop, coupled with inadequate food and ill-heated homes, lack of medicines and inability to afford to call a doctor, could so easily bring on a chill leading to galloping pneumonia and sudden death within a few days. Heart attacks and strokes, in the absence of free medical treatment and "miracle" drugs were commonplace in launching people into eternity. Labourers fell off scaffolding and machine mincers got trapped in unguarded machinery because few protective measures were required by law. Such frailties bred a generation conscious that it must take care. We were much more aware of the hazards around us and were not surrounded by protective measures as we are today. We learned how to circumvent the more obvious dangers. If we did not look after ourselves and mishaps befell there was no-one else would.

"All For Each and Each For All"

One evening in the late 1920s Mrs Bradford called unexpectedly. We had known Mrs Bradford for some time. Her husband worked with my father and we met on most summer Saturday afternoons at Kynoch's sports field where the menfolk played bowls, the women chatted and we played with their children, but her mission that evening had nothing to do with Kynoch's or its sports field, but was to encourage the formation of a Women's Co-operative Guild at Perry Common. It was a mission that led us into fresh fields where we made many friends.

Mrs Bradford was the Treasurer of the Guild at Witton and had been deputed to try to form a similar one on the new estate. In the 1920s and 1930s the Co-operative Movement exercised considerable influence on life in the city. Its motto "All for each and each for all" had a practical appeal. A dividend was paid to Co-operative shareholders, the customers, at shops and they were encouraged to take part in its educational and social activities. It was a peaceful and progressive movement. Politics there were, but they were the politics of hope, encouragement and achievement. There were several city councillors and members of Parliament who first cut their teeth with the Co-operative Movement.

My brother and I listened to all this, although ostensibly reading our comics in the corner to which we had been banished so that Mrs Bradford could enjoy the fireside. The object of her visit was to persuade my mother to help with the formation of a Women's Guild at Perry Common. There were no clubs, or even pubs, where people could meet. It was a social and cultural desert, and the idea of a weekly social meeting with educational and recreational objectives made an instant appeal to our mother, who had always been conscious of the deprivations inflicted on the working classes. She had experienced many vicissitudes in her early life.

Her father had died before she was born, and when she was eighteen her mother had died, leaving her in a world where the only respectable employment for a young girl was in service. She had progressed from a children's nursemaid with a "well-to do" family in Dudley to that of a lady's maid to the wife of the American Consul in Birmingham. She had travelled with her employers on several occasions and in 1912 narrowly missed becoming a victim on the ill-starred "Titanic."

She had experienced far more than most women of her generation and her encounters had made her deeply conscious of what she felt to be injustices in society which we, in our comfortable home, found difficult to appreciate. We listened fascinated to her stories of brave suffragettes who had fought for equal voting rights with men, and of broken promises made during the Great War of homes and secure jobs for the returning soldiers. Only that year had many women now approaching middle age become entitled to vote. In our parents' opinion the working classes had been duped. Strikes had been crushed and any attempts at peaceful discussion by the ill-equipped trades unions had been doomed. The days of an assertive workforce lay years ahead.

The upshot of Mrs Bradford's visit was the formation of a branch of the Guild at Perry Common which met each week in one of the schoolrooms opposite. There was nowhere else to meet. Our mother became its first president; a position she held for many years.

The pleasure she got from her new-found interest, which amounted to something akin to a crusade at times, was reflected in our own enjoyment. We joined a junior class where we had games and competitions, interspersed with subtle propaganda, tales of the Rochdale Pioneers and visits to the Co-operative dairy, bakery and other establishments. There was the annual Co-operators Day in July with its procession of decorated floats.

On one of these days I was cajoled into playing a part on the coalman's cart, hastily converted in the yard behind the Co-op shops to present a tableau portraying Co-op confectionery. The float's centrepiece was a huge cardboard wedding cake, surrounded by a group of juvenile wedding guests with me, in a morning suit borrowed from a midget known to one of the Guild members, as the groom. It seemed a long and gruelling journey behind a reluctant horse to join the main procession through the city centre and thence to Ward End Park for further celebrations. Then there was Children's Day in August, when the whole of the amusement park at Sutton Park was taken over for sports, tea and entertainment for thousands of members children. It was for many the only holiday they had.

Guild night was always on Wednesdays when we were left with our father. Our mother never missed a meeting or any of the periodic social events. On these occasions we were allowed to stay up later to be entertained by our father who was adept at concocting mechanical wonders from scraps of wood, cardboard and metal; little dancing men with jointed limbs made from sawn-off clothes pegs, a maze of holes, inclines and declines through which marbles could be rolled, puppets or peep shows in an old shoe box. Sometimes we helped with his photography, developing and print-ing in the tiny "bogey hole" beneath the stairs, or he would mystify us with conjuring tricks.

One evening he produced two toothed metal strips that could be joined together by pulling a metal tab along them. It was a specimen of something about to go into production in a new division at Kynoch's. He called it a "lightning fastener". It intrigued and fascinated us because we could not see how it worked or what it could possibly be used for, but this little novelty was a prototype of an invention destined to revolutionise the fastenings on clothing.

Sometimes, if in a lyrical mood, our father would light his pipe from a wooden spill taken from a brass shell case he had made during the war, and which now served as a spill can. He began:

'Twas in the prime of summer time
An evening calm and cool,

>   And four-and-twenty happy boys
>   Came bounding out of school

. . . and recited the whole of *Eugene Aram* or another of Hood's poems without recourse to the book. He was very fond of narrative poems, as was our mother who could recite Browning's *Pied Piper of Hamelin* without missing a stanza, and we were frequently reminded of how Horatius kept the bridge "against such fearful odds" but never on Wednesday evenings when she was far too busy pursuing the ideals of the Guild. By 1930 she had progressed to becoming a member of the Executive Committee, represented the Society at its Cheltenham conference, and subsequently acted as a hostess to delegates at the Birmingham conference. 1931 saw the celebration of fifty years of achievement. At a two-week exhibition Bingley Hall was filled with working exhibits and tableaux illustrating the Society's work. There were street processions, events at the Botanical Gardens with fireworks and inspiring speeches in the Town Hall.

Locally many extension activities were developed. There were dressmaking and leathercraft classes, a choir and drama group. All of these provided diversions for the wives who lived on the estate. They were able to escape from their toils to find enlightenment and relaxation in these activities.

Inevitably we made many friends among the members' children; friendships that lasted through adolescence. Of these, Maurice, son of one of my mother's friends, became the closest. He developed a pleasing tenor voice and we spent many hours round the piano with the other members of his family with whom we became deeply involved. We had much in common and later, as adolescence dawned, we discussed many things on our Sunday morning walks across Sutton Park; politics, books, music, religion, love; but death was not one of them. It lay too far in the future. There were troubles in Spain, China and Palestine, and a foreign king was assassinated in France, but these were all in far away countries. We had not heard of Hitler or Mussolini. No coming events cast their shadows. They lay beyond the horizon and the time when many of our generation would be scattered around the globe, some never to return. We were hardly gilded youth but those few years in the 1930s were golden ones.

As with many organisations the Co-operative Movement expressed its hopes in a song which floated across from the school as we went to bed.

England arise, the long, long night is over.
England arise for the day is here.

It was tantamount to an anthem and full of expectation. As we grew older we were allowed to attend some of the social events, variously called an American supper, a conversazione or simply a social. There was little to detect between them except that salmon sandwiches were served at American suppers but not at the other events. We had to sit at the back of the hall and not be a nuisance, which was ensured by a Mrs Dobson. She had no children of her own but assumed responsibility for the behaviour of those of others. We were not slow to goad her with roguish high spirits, but before we could relish the refreshments prepared by members we had to enjoy or endure the entertainments. Our intentions, like those that paved the way to hell, were good, but we were not always appreciative of the efforts of those who sought to entertain. They titillated a warped sense of schoolboy humour that was not malicious but wickedly mischievous, and our mimicry and mockery were typical of those on the threshold of adolescence when everything amused and life was fun.

Some Guild members were talented, others who imagined they were produced a levity that was difficult to control and had to be suppressed with handkerchieves stuffed into our mouths. Encouraged by each other the furtive hilarity was irrepressible. We had to turn away to stifle the merriment, only to be confronted by the gaunt, angular figure of Mrs Dobson, who had taken a stance at the rear of the hall with the sole idea of maintaining discipline. Her sharp features developed a frown and she advanced, casting a glare of censure and pointing a menacing finger from her claw-like hand. The combination was sometimes too much and refuge had to be sought in the sanctuary of the cloakrooms to relieve our mirth.

From time to time guest artistes appeared. They sang the same songs from a limited repertoire. Mrs Devonshire was a regular visitor; well-built and always clad in a long brown garment she called her "gown". She sang, one hand supporting her sheet of music, the other her ample bosom, beguiling her audience with her aspirations to "rest close to his breast under the deodar" or quavering over "where my caravan has rested." We were so convulsed by her gestures, the intermittent jangles of her bangles and the swirls of her pearls as they fell over the precipice of her bosom that we never did discover what befell under the deodar or even what it was, any more than learning where her caravan finally came to rest.

Another memorable artiste was a Mrs Roughwoode, a semi-professional, who liked to be introduced as "Madame" Roughwoode. She had a deep, rich contralto voice, and her costume and jewellery seemed to conflict with her intonation that she was "less than the dust beneath thy chariot wheels." Rehearsals for the one-act plays that were to be presented at the drama festivals were always taken seriously. There was no sniggering and these simple plays aroused an interest in the live theatre.

After the refreshment interval there was usually dancing to the piano played by Mrs Dobson, which restricted her supervision of irrepressible children. It was not so important at this stage because, as there were no male partners for the Guild ladies, the boys were reluctantly dragged onto the floor to be joggled around beneath the sagging bosoms of hearty females determined to teach us the waltz or the foxtrot to the tunes of *Springtime in the Rockies*, *Bye bye Blackbird* or other popular tunes of the era. "You must learn to dance if you are to get anywhere" these convivial ladies crooned as they swept us around the floor .

On winter Saturday evenings, and before many people had wireless sets or made a habit of visiting the cinema once the "talkies" had arrived, whist drives were arranged. As we were not old enough to be left at home nor old enough to join in the game, we were usually allocated a couple of tables in a corner where we were initiated into various simple card games by those adults not engaged in the whist drive.

The most enjoyable events were the "Grand Concerts" which were organised more professionally than the week night socials. The concerts were always held on Saturday evenings. Most of the Guild members knew of some talented amateurs who were glad of an opportunity to exercise their abilities. Mr Alf Tipp, who worked with my father, could usually be persuaded to take part. He had a fine tenor voice, worthy of the operatic stage, but in the context of the era, there was little hope of this. He had to be content with a production line job and realise his potential at local concerts.

His powerful rendering of *Song of Songs* and *You are my Heart's Delight* needed no microphone to charge the atmosphere with emotion. There were vocal duets, *The Battle Eve*, *Excelsior* and *The Two Gendarmes*, piano recitals and dramatic recitations; *The Green Eye of the Little Yellow God* and others recounting sensational shipwrecks, battles or melodramatic rides across sun-scorched deserts where the horsemen died of thirst.

Conjurors and ventriloquists could usually be found to provide a balanced programme which invariably ended with the community singing of nostalgic wartime songs. *Keep the Home Fires Burning*, *There's a Long, Long Trail a Winding* and other stimulators of damp handker-chieves that aroused in us an uncomfortable feeling of sadness. "We sang those songs during the war," said Mrs

Moore, looking wistfully at her husband, whose eyes seemed to look beyond her to the fields of Flanders. Miss Gatesenby dabbed her eyes. Was she, perhaps, seeing again in the casualty lists a young man's name? Whatever the reason she remained a spinster, but it was now time for us to help with the clearing away of chairs and preparing the hall for Monday morning's school assembly.

For our generation these events, enjoyed through our mother's preoccupation with the Co-operative Movement, were joyous occasions that cost little or nothing and, among our parents as a new decade dawned, there seemed to be fresh hope that the long-promised new world lay just around the corner. The war was more than ten years behind, there was no thought of another one and life, if hardly serene was, for most of us, comfortable within our parents' means. For them things had not always been so enjoyable The critical shortage of suitable housing at the end of the First World War had forced them to spend the first seven years of their marriage in the far less salubrious environment of a mid-Victorian courtyard sharing a home with an aunt.

Cottages for Artisans

It was not the sound of carriage wheels scraping on the gravel drive or the voice of a maid chatting to the postman that greeted my earliest waking moments. The noises I heard were less refined; the grinding and clanging of the trams as they trundled up Wheeler Street past the end of the entry that led from the courtyard into the street and the clatter of the milkman's pail as he shouted "Milkyo." He banged on doors with a metal ladle he used to pour foaming milk from his pail into the the jugs produced by the housewives in response to his knock.

Wheeler Street was long and straight, steep and narrow. It isn't anymore. Inner city ring roads have cut across it and tower blocks have obscured a view that was once dramatic but hardly pleasing. The street began near the summit of Constitution Hill and overshadowed by the lofty embattled tower of Saint George's Church which became a casualty amid the rising blocks of post-1945 development. It swept down to where the slender spire of Saint Matthias's Church alone broke the monotony of continuous roof lines and smoking chimneys, and then upwards to the heights of Lozells to terminate at the foot of Saint Paul's Church tower.

Such a prospect could have delighted the architect who transformed the Paris of Napoleon III. He might have visualised an opportunity to create a thoroughfare of monumental proportions with a focal point at each end, but the speculative builders of Birmingham in the middle of the nineteenth century were not concerned with creating majestic boulevards with magnificent vistas but with satisfying the urgent need of accommodation for the thousands flocking into the town in the aftermath of the Industrial Revolution. Their attempts reflected little credit on them or on the back-to-back houses euphemistically described as "cottages for artisans", they built around squalid courtyards at a time when building regulations were either non-existent or disregarded.

The trams that ran the length of Wheeler Street set it apart from surrounding ones, and the shops that had appeared lent it an air that was slightly superior to that of the surrounding streets. It was a place where people congregated at tram stops and in and around the shops. Such prestige was enhanced by the destination indicators on the trams which made it known that a Number 24 travelled to Lozells "via Wheeler Street".

In the 1920s nine out of ten Birmingham families lived in rented accommodation owned by private landlords. It was the natural order. To own a home was the privilege of the wealthy. How could anyone from the working classes accumulate sufficient money to buy a house and pay for its maintenance, repairs and insurance? The idea was as remote as that of wives going out to work. The Great War (as it continued to be called until overtaken by a later one) had left thousands without a home of their own, and living with relatives in cramped quarters, in lodgings or rooms with neighbours.

This desperate housing shortage had forced my mother and father, who had married in 1919, to take the only accommodation available to them with a maiden aunt who lived in a tiny house in a courtyard sympathetically named Martha Place that lay behind Number 56 Wheeler Street. It was to be a temporary arrangement until one of the homes promised by the politicians during the late war materialised. The temporary period was to last for seven years in the restless world of unemployment, strikes, rising prices, and the international turmoil and ferment into which I was born, protected from the worst effects of the bitterness and in ignorance of the strife for many years. Some of the impressions of those early years spent in a house rented for six shillings and eleven pence (35p) stand out with photographic clarity, others remain vague and uncertain.

Martha Place was gained through a narrow entry next to a greengrocer's. The conditions in the courtyard were not as sordid as those endured in many others. Each house in Martha Place had a WC and a small garden of some fourteen feet by ten. Two wash houses provided cold water taps, a brick wash boiler and a stoneware sink for the six families that lived in the courtyard houses. Our mother and father had been accustomed to better accommodation in Victorian suburban villas but, as with most people at that time, they determined to make the best of things until a government, grateful for their efforts during the war, kept its promise of somewhere else to live. For the time being they had a home of their own which was superior to many in other courts where there were no gardens and several families had to share a privy and one tap in the yard.

Oblivious of the deficiencies, my brother and I took for granted the warmth and affection inside the tiny house, crammed with furniture in anticipation of more spacious accommodation and where routine was paramount. The furniture was polished, china and brass-ware gleamed and reflected the flames that danced in a huge fireplace where a kettle sang and puffed all day long. A grandfather clock, still in the family, stood, sentinel-like, in a corner. Above its dial a painted moon rose, waxed, waned and then disappeared with the lunar phases. In its wake a painted galleon rode across a wild and stormy sea. On a nearby table stood a handwound gramophone with a large trumpet-shaped horn. The sounds that came out were volume-controlled by stuffing a piece of velvet into the horn. An Irish shillelagh, a souvenir of our father's only visit abroad, hung over the door. At the rear of the living room another door opened into a dark vestibule and a spiral wooden staircase that ascended to a bedroom and an attic and a brick one that descended to a cellar lit only by an iron grating used for deliveries of coal.

Despite its shortcomings, Martha Place at that time was a homely place where joys and sorrows were shared and help was always at hand; a microcosm of courtyard society where there was tacit agreement over the use of the two wash houses by the six households. The conditions in the Victorian courtyards were accepted, albeit with reluctance and resignation, by a generation whose memory was still fresh from the horrors of the trenches during the late war. The soldiers had not returned to the land of milk and honey they had been promised but it was early days. They had endured much worse and things were sure to improve. The politicians had told them so.

As a child I developed a gradual awareness of others who lived in Martha Place. At first they were but shadows that passed by the window or bent to chuckle over a pram, but identification of faces, clothes and mannerisms was soon established.

At the house furthest from ours and at right angles to it lived Mrs Hancocks and her two sons. She was a war widow who took in washing. She did some of ours, not from reluctance to launder on our mother's part but out of sympathy for a war widow trying to supplement her pension. Next to her lived a Mrs Evans, also a widow, and with her lived another old lady. She was probably not more than sixty but to my brother and me she seemed very old. She was known only as "Ryah". It was certainly not Mrs Ryah and was assumed to be a corruption of Maria.

She was always clad in the same long navy-coloured skirt of voluminous proportions and a grey shawl which she clutched tightly round her throat. Her head was crowned with a man's cloth cap; a custom of many older Birmingham women of the labouring classes in those days. Totally without teeth, her hooked nose and chin protruded beyond her shrunken gums and lent to her profile the appearance of a half-opened pair of nut crackers. In a pair of shapeless buttoned boots she would shuffle past our window in the early evening clasping an empty jug. A little later she returned with the jug overflowing with a frothy concoction. In answer to a child's curiosity came the answer that it was Ryah's medicine.

One evening she failed to return from her mysterious mission until a sudden scream and the squeal of the brakes of a tram from the bottom of the entry sent those within earshot to ascertain the cause. It transpired that Ryah had dropped her brimming jug and, in her efforts to retrieve the remains, had slipped off the pavement and into the path of an oncoming tramcar. It was many years before we learnt the true nature of Ryah's nightly errands and her addiction to the "demon drink" that had almost caused a fatality.

At the next house, and with two older daughters, lived a Mrs Logan. She was also a war widow who startled us early one evening when she knocked on the door asking to borrow a walking stick to help one of her daughters, who seemed to be in a very distressed state, to get to the tram. It was some days later that she returned carrying a baby. Once more it was many years before the full facts of the case became apparent. Immorality was not condoned and the stigma attached to the girl who bore the shame and the mother the blame, led to their eventual disappearance. Such an event would create little ferment nowadays but, in those days and even in the courtyards, there were, for the majority, rigid standards over what was done and what was not done. The occupants of the last house in the block of four were a Mr and Mrs Moseley. Both were very old and had no children. Mrs Moseley always appeared clad in long black clothes of pre-war vintage, a cloak and a Victorian bonnet tied under her chin. Not endowed with very good eyesight, she found her way by banging on the walls with a stick. To us, and inspired by gruesome fairy stories, she appeared as a witch personified.

The only other occupants of Martha Place were Mrs Wilkes and her two young sons who ran the street-facing greengrocers shop onto which their house backed. Her husband had also died as a result, we suspected, of injuries sustained in the terrible war of which we gradually became aware from overheard conversations that perturbed us. It had been caused by someone called "The Kaiser" and some quite dreadful people called Germans. Mr Moseley apart, our father who had been released from conscription to become employed making shells and cartridges at Kynoch's ammunition factory, was the only man among the inhabitants of Martha Place.

We saw little of our father during the week. Long before we were up he had departed for his work as an engineer's turner, but as we grew older, we were allowed to go to the bottom of the entry each evening. to watch for him alighting from the tram.

There was little variation in daily routine, except on the afternoons we were taken to Handsworth Park in my mother's hope of finding there clearer air than that of our immediate surroundings. She sometimes shopped on the way at Knight's grocery shop where our custom was often rewarded with a biscuit. The shop floor was congested with sacks from which Mr Knight extracted sugar, tea and dried fruit which he weighed in little blue bags on a pair of brass scales. Nearby was the sawdust-covered floor of the butcher's where, to relieve the tedium of waiting, we shuffled our small feet.

Opposite was an intriguing shop known as "the huckster's" which sold saucepans, buckets, kettles, brushes and brooms and other vital commodities rarely needed today; gas mantles, oil lamps, wicks, paraffin and candles. Each shop had its own distinctive aroma, none more so than that of the newsagents on the corner of Bridge Street and kept by two spinsters; the Misses Gillott. It was approached by steep stone steps, worn uneven by generations of customers. Their shop floor was covered with linoleum so old and cracked that it no longer lay flat, but bubbled and curled against the shop counter when we trod on it. The smell inside the shop was one of fresh newsprint, musty floor covering and the aniseed balls and troach drops with which the Misses Gillott sought to increase their takings.

From time to time we were taken further afield; to Evans and Evans, a kind of suburban department store "upon the Lozells" as that highly-esteemed shopping centre was called, in quest of haberdashery and hairpins. Sometimes it was "down at the Brook" at Hockley, where there was no sign of a brook that had long ago been put into a culvert. Such was the quaint terminology in vogue that an inspection of ribbons and cottons at Norton's Emporium entailed going "down on the Flat" as the region at the foot of Key Hill was called.

Time spent indoors was accompanied by the droning and clattering of the passing trams that vibrated the houses and rattled the crockery to the extent that visitors whose teacups had not been filled to the brim were overheard to remark good-humouredly "It looks as if the tram's just gone by."

There was a permanency about the trams. There were few buses then — no more than a dozen routes — but the trams had always been there. They were ubiquitous and ran along all the city's main arteries, and the inner suburbs were honeycombed with a maze of tracks and overhead wiring.

New routes were still being built in the 1920s; most of them along reserved tracks to the developing suburbs. These were served by a new batch of fully-enclosed bogie cars that were superior to those that ran along Wheeler Street, which were old four-wheelers relegated from more prosperous routes. They had exposed driver's platforms and open balconies on the top decks, but the lower saloons were resplendent with elaborately-carved woodwork and lights enclosed in little pink glass shades. At each end a sliding door bore the symbol of the Municipal Bank; a key engraved in the frosted glass.

The passengers sat, backs to the windows, on longitudinal wooden benches punctured with fretwork designs and had been so highly polished by the bottoms of travellers that a sudden deceleration precipitated passengers towards the front of the car. The trams, solid and immutable, ran at appointed times, on fixed tracks and in all weathers. When impenetrable fogs engulfed the city they forged along forewarning anyone ahead with the driver's gong, and when the snow had fallen so heavily that other vehicles could make no progress, the trams, with snowploughs attached, cleared a pathway for them. The trams were as imperishable as the tracks upon which they ran — or so we thought.

Of all the sounds that reverberated through the streets none had more impact on the lives of the local population than that of the "bull", as the siren mounted on the roof of Lucas's factory in nearby Great King Street was called. The seven o'clock bull woke people up, and at five minutes to eight it reminded the workmen that they had five minutes to get inside the factory gates before they clanged shut. There was a mid-day bull and one at "knocking off time" in the evening which sent housewives scurrying home. The influence of the bull was all-pervading. It regulated people's lives. It sent people scuttling, either to work or home. Those who had them set their watches by it and adjusted their clocks. Those who had neither relied on it to remind them of the passage of time and conversations were frequently punctuated with "I must get home before the bull goes," "I'll wait until the bull goes" and a dilatory woman would excuse her procrastination with the excuse that she "didn't hear the bull". Only on Saturday afternoons when the workforce had gone home and on Sundays did the bull fall silent.

An ever-widening circle of relatives, friends and acquaintances in those early years influenced our attitudes and behaviour, and overheard conversations affected our thinking. Except for weekend visits we saw little of the menfolk. They were either at work or, if on night shift, in bed.

Aunts there were in profusion and, like the lords

spiritual and temporal, were of two breeds; those of the blood, the "real" ones who lived in the Black Country and were seen less often than those friends of our mother who were "aunts" by courtesy. This plethora of aunts was further subdivided into the many who were lovable and fun-loving and the few who were gaunt and forbidding.

Into the latter category fell Aunt Nellie "Smethwick" (which distinguished her from her jolly fun-loving namesake who lived in Selly Oak) and to whom visits were dreaded. Her conversation was limited to insipid platitudes and gratuitous advice to small boys. She seemed to enjoy neither good health nor bad; her condition she invariably described as "middling".

Apart from a brief interval to prepare tea, she would sit before the fire clicking her knitting needles, like Madame Defarge before the guillotine, deploring the state of the country or the behaviour of young people, pausing only to massage her toothless gums by alternately pursing and sucking her lips. My brother and I were quick to mimic her when out of earshot, but it was through these friends and our mother's sociability that we got to know other parts of the city when we were taken to visit on trams through streets that throbbed with activity and interest to homes in Cannon Hill, Selly Oak, Small Heath, Kings Heath and even as far as Bournville and Hall Green.

Most of the aunts lived in houses that, compared with ours, seemed vast, although they were modest Victorian villas or terraced houses. They all seemed to have a great deal of unused accommodation and comprised a scullery, a kitchen, what was called "the middle room" originally intended as, but rarely used for, a dining room and a front parlour. Family life and entertaining centred on the kitchen which was the only room where a bright fire burned. Curiosity and sometimes boredom led my brother and me to explore beyond the door leading from the kitchen along a stone-flagged passage past cellar steps, a pantry, stairs, closets and eventually to the front parlour where only on winter Sunday afternoons and at Christmas was a fire ever lit to burn reluctantly into a damp chimney.

Within this hallowed chamber blinds were kept half-drawn to prevent any penetrating sunbeams from fading the furniture and carpets. The room exuded a damp and musty smell. Photographs of people long departed gazed down from the walls on the bric-a-brac that cluttered a chiffonier and bamboo tables. The atmosphere was not conducive to lingering, even to satisfy a child's curiosity. "Come out and shut it up, quick," commanded the gaunt and disagreeable Aunt Nellie who had steamed up the passage behind us in sombre grey dress like a dreadnought chasing the enemy. She bore down on us with guns blazing as we were discovered invading forbidden territory. "Don't you ever go in there again," she remonstrated.

We retreated crestfallen to the nether regions. Neither sunlight, fresh air nor curious youngsters, it seemed, must disturb a room designed not to be lived in but to be preserved as a shrine. At some homes we visited for years we never penetrated beyond the door that led from the kitchen to the passage and could only speculate over what lay beyond. Whether or not central heating would have made any difference to the pattern of life we shall never know, but there was a shocking waste of living space badly needed by families that huddled round a fireside in a kitchen so crowded that one of our young friends likened theirs to the Black Hole of Calcutta.

One aunt we did not visit was Aunt Jane because she lived with us. She was my mother's step-sister by an earlier marriage of my grandmother, and was ten years her senior. She had always been there and, in many respects, took the place of grandparents. She was a diminutive figure scarcely five feet in height but her rounded shoulders made her look even less, and her pale grey eyes seemed to be engaged in a perpetual search for pennies that might have been dropped on the ground. She continued to wear her hair scraped up all round into an Edwardian top knot long after our mother had abandoned the style for the more up-to-date one of a Grecian bun worn at the nape of the neck.

Our parents occasionally went to the theatre or the cinema. Sometimes they went into town, at other times to the *Metropole*, a converted theatre at the foot of Constitution Hill, but more usually to the *Villa Cross*, newly built for film projection, where, in more superior surroundings and the company of audiences from Handsworth, they could enjoy the silent exploits of Mary Pickford, Douglas Fairbanks, Rudolph Valentino and other screen idols. On such occasions we were left in the care of Aunt Jane who would regale us with tales of relatives who had sailed across the seas in search of a better life and of those who had perished in colliery disasters. While she told her tales her fingers would sometimes be engaged in slicing thin strips from a block of wood into spills which my father used to light his pipe from the fire and so save matches or she would engage herself in making a hearth rug from pieces of cloth she had cut from discarded clothing and "pegging" them into a piece of hessian. "The Devil finds work for idle hands," she interspersed into her narrative.

Aunt Jane had been sparsely educated for a penny a week. Born before the compulsory Education Act she had been taught to read and write, but little else, at a Dame's school and always found difficulty in reading and pronouncing words of more than three syllables and was sometimes gently chided for using unfamiliar Black Country words. She "pared" potatoes and ate her meals with a "prong", but she more than compensated for her lack of command of the vernacular with the sweeping gestures she used to press home a point. No fork ever carried a lighter load than hers but she wielded it at the dinner table with the dexterity of a swordsman to emphasise a declaration and frequently had to be physically restrained to prevent bodily harm when her arms, like the sails of a windmill, flailed the air.

She was employed as the cook at Bridge Street Police Station and, from what she related, was unceasingly teased by the sergeant and his men. She had the faith of a child and allowed herself to be locked in a police cell on one occasion and handcuffed on another. "But they took them off so that I could cook their dinner," she said.

If it were possible to act contrary to expectation Aunt would do so. If the clocks had to be advanced or retarded she invariably did the opposite. She frequently got onto trams going the wrong way or overshot her station when travelling by train, and all because she would not ask. But there was one event for which I was grateful for her propensity to become confused.

Bostock and Wombwell's "Wild Beast Show" was in town and it was suggested that Aunt Jane might like to take me. It was a show I was destined never to see. Arriving at the venue she rummaged in the capacious handbag in which she kept what she called her "tranklements" (which included her smelling salts in a green-stoppered bottle that never failed to fascinate) and extracted the money demanded at a cash desk before we were ushered into a darkened auditorium. After a few minutes wait, some curtains parted and a lady began to tinkle the keys of a piano as black and white pictures flickered across a screen. Even to a five-year old it became obvious that this was no wild beast show but some kind of "moving pictures" we heard our parents talk about but, having paid to come in, Aunt would admit to no mistake. The main film must have been of poor quality and so scratched that it seemed to be con-tinually raining. The highlight for me was the antics of a black and white cat who, despite earthquakes and being blown-up by dynamite, "kept on walking still".

There were smiles when we returned and a mild berating by my father for having taken me to a "flea pit" at Gosta Green. But for Aunt's unpredictable behaviour I should never have seen a silent film nor the escapades of Felix the imperishable cat. By the time I was old enough to be taken to a cinema both had been super-seded by the "talkies" and Walt Disney's mouse.

Winter routine varied from that of the rest of the year only that my brother and I were stationed at the window at dusk to listen for the footfalls of the lamplighter echoing along the entry. He carried a long pole which he raised to the gas lamp in the courtyard. At the touch of his wand, the flickering gas light transformed the court-yard, mellowing its drabness with a pale glow. It was time to draw the living room curtains and hold a match to the incandescent gas mantle; an inverted cup of asbestos netting at the bottom of a rigid pipe that hung from the ceiling. The brightness of the light could be adjusted by pulling one of the chains that hung on either side and operated a butterfly valve that regulated the gas supplied from a "penny in the slot" meter. A fading flame and a cry of "The gas is going" was a forewarning that another penny was needed.

This was the time, just before tea, that an interest in music was aroused as we listened to the tinkling tunes from the Gilbert and Sullivan operas that came from the horn of the gramophone, or to our mother singing as she accompanied herself on her Neapolitan mandolin. Sometimes Aunt Jane would read to us. She had but two books; treasured school prizes lovingly covered with brown paper, and which she read time and again. From one, and before I was five years old, I had followed the progress of Christian and his friend, Faithful, through the Slough of Despond and the Valley of the Shadow of Death, but in ignorance of the allegorical nature of

81

Bunyan's *Pilgrim's Progress*. Her other book was a morbid Victorian tale, *Little Dot.*

It told of a child preoccupied with an unnatural curiosity over death, who spent her days in the gruesome surroundings of a churchyard listening to the vapourings of an aged gravedigger as he excavated sites from which to launch victims into eternity. They were all, naturally, very suitable candidates for heaven and made their exits via edifying deathbeds, Little Dot among them. Our mother did not approve of such pathos, preferring to divert us with the highly moral tales from *Struwelpeter*, subtitled *Merry Stories and Funny Pictures*. Anything less merry would be hard to imagine. They were frightening stories of the fates that befell children who refused their soup (they died), sucked their thumbs (they were cut off), or played with matches (they were burned to death), but the stories were no doubt read with good moral intent before we were ushered upstairs to further our acquaintance with God and Jesus, who had come early into our lives in a simple prayer repeated kneeling at the bedside:-

> Gentle Jesus meek and mild,
> Look upon a little child.
> Pity my simplicity,
> Suffer me to come to thee.

At the end of this invocation we were requested to use a chamber pot withdrawn from beneath the bed. There seemed to be some inexplicable connection between

God, the prayer and the pot to which God suffered us to come before being allowed into bed.

At mealtimes there was a similar ritual when a "Thank you for what we have just received amen please may I get down?" gabbled in a single sentence was a routine chant that permitted us to leave the table. It was all very confusing. Who was this God and his Jesus we could not see but who saw all, heard all, knew all and "moved in a mysterious way"? They existed of course, and we knew from simple hymns that they lived "above the clear blue sky in heaven's bright abode." The skies above Birmingham were rarely clear blue, but there were times when I contemplated God's abode through the window in the hope that I might glimpse his face peering earthwards from between the scudding clouds. If these early aspirations achieved nothing else, they instilled a code of behaviour in the sure belief that any misdemeanours would bring about the wrath of the Almighty.

One morning there was an uncanny silence. The bull did not sound and the quickening footsteps of men hurrying to work did not echo along the entry. No trams clattered by and the street was strangely silent. Going downstairs we saw that our father had not gone off to work but, as usual, Aunt Jane was putting on her hat ready to leave for the Police Station. "Strike or no strike," she declared, "I'm going to get the policemen's dinners!"

Clearly there was something amiss. It was the first day of the General Strike of 1926. There was some talk between the grown-ups about miners and train drivers wanting more money, and of lockouts and blacklegs, but it didn't mean much to us although our parents tried to explain what it was all about. Aunt Jane's return in the evening brought the intelligence that the policemen's sergeant (our only source of news as there were no newspapers) expected that someone called Mr Baldwin would do something, but the lamplighter, who seemed of greater concern to him, would do nothing.

The strike continued. It made little impact on our lives. We were fed, the fire continued to burn and the grandfather clock ticked on, until one day, and for a reason long forgotten, my father found it necessary to go into town. He took me with him. "We shall have to walk because there are no trams running," he said. We set off along an almost deserted street and, as we approached Constitution Hill there was a hissing along the overhead tram wires that warned of an approaching tram. This rounded the corner at an alarming speed, propelled not by a uniformed driver but by several young men in civilian clothes. Rocking perilously over some points and dropping sand that created a shower of sparks, the tram disappeared over the brow of the hill. In answer to my doubts over there being no trams, my father replied that this was not a "proper one" and was driven by a group of university students.

With confidence in his unfailing honesty restored, the expedition was accomplished without further incident. What remained of that week, however, was a period of feverish activity and excitement. Furniture was moved around and drawers and cupboards were emptied and their erstwhile contents packed into boxes. Down from the attic came trunks filled with books, and up from the cellar came a workbench and my father's tools. Whether or not all this activity was connected to the visit to town I shall now never know, but our parents elation told that it had nothing to do with the General Strike. We had been allocated a brand new council house.

So we left the "artisan's cottage" in Martha Place, all traces of which have been obliterated. The street where it stood has been re-aligned and trees shade the greensward that has replaced the cobblestones where horses hooves and trams once clattered. It would be difficult to pinpoint exactly where Martha Place once stood and, but for the incident of the over-eager volunteer tram drivers and the move to new surroundings, there would have been no memories of the General Strike that caused so much suffering and bitterness.

Preaching and Teaching

The prospects for an enjoyable Sunday were dismal. The Sabbath, according to the scriptures and supported by the law, was a rest day, except for our mothers who spent most of it preparing, serving and clearing away meals. Sunday routine was set in tablets of stone. Legislation prevented theatres, cinemas and shops from opening their doors and sports that were legitimate on the six working days were illegal or at least immoral on the seventh. Until the early 1930s we had no wireless set so, unless one was an avid reader, the day could only be spent in contemplation of the next one. Reading was restricted to bound books. Comics were not allowed, and any attempt to discover the reasoning behind this was dismissed with "Because it is Sunday." There was a rarified quality in the binding of a book that placed its contents above suspicion but comics, which could be read with impunity on weekdays became objects of corruption on Sundays. Paperback novels, had they existed, would have posed problems because of the intangible connection between unbound literature and iniquity.

God and his spokesman, Jesus, put irrational restraints on our Sunday activities. Games played on weekdays and involving dice or cards were deemed to be vice-ridden on Sundays and were not permitted. This also applied to ball games, which ruled out a whole host of those involving the use of a sphere that lost its honour on the Sabbath. The streets fell silent. There was no playing there and loud laughter in the garden was frowned upon, but this was probably because it was likely to disturb slumbering fathers who, by a long-established Birmingham custom, retired to bed after the mid-day meal until three o'clock. For this reason it was considered discourteous to visit for tea earlier than halfpast three. To dance or sing, other than hymns or songs of a religious nature was an indication of the depths of depravity.

Adult activities were also curbed. Few men would have indulged in manual hobbies and the womenfolk would not have been found sewing or knitting. There had been a suspension of the ban on knitting during the war, presumably with the Almighty's approval, provided that it was being done for the soldiers. The temporary suspension was rescinded immediately the war ended. No-one would have thought of hanging out washing on Sundays for fear of censure.

Religion and superstition influenced most people's lives. It was an era of uncertainty when portents, premonitions and predictions were regarded seriously and *Old Moore's Almanack* was studied assiduously. We became acquainted with this publication through Aunt Jane, who came for the day on most Sundays. She awaited its arrival with eager anticipation. "Old Moore's due next week" she said, creating the impression that Old Moore himself came to donate her a personal copy. Mother Shipton's prophesies and predictions were not unheeded. This irrational fear of the unknown persisted in the aftermath of the Victorian era and manifested itself in absurd superstitions. Thirteen people would not have sat down together for a meal for it was certain that one of them would die before the year ended. Knives appearing crossed on a table indicated an impending quarrel. Aunt Jane attacked a gaping hole in the coal fire vigorously because it indicated a terrible fate for a member of the family. No-one would deliberately walk under a ladder, and coming face to face with a cross-eyed person, seeing a piebald horse, or the new moon through glass unnerved people who went in dread of the consequences.

Not to attend church at least once on Sunday was unthinkable to many. It was putting the promise of eternal life at risk and even in times of adversity the majority of people felt that they had much to be thankful for. Not to acknowledge this at Sunday worship was tantamount to inciting the wrath of an avenging God. Even the non-churchgoers felt it advisable to send their children as intermediaries. It was also a convenient way of getting them out of the way for an hour or so.

The morning service we were forced to attend was a formal occasion. Few grown-ups attended because domestic duties took precedence. The "Morning Service" from the *Book of Common Prayer* was strictly adhered to and necessitated wearing one's Sunday best clothes. A fear of damaging them precluded any larking about on the way to and from Saint Martin's Church, but this was counterbalanced by a certain amount of surreptitious horseplay during the sermon by God's envoy, the Reverend Harris, who demanded an excessive amount of time acknowledging our "manifold sins and wicked-ness", repenting on our behalf and asking forgiveness of a merciful God who seemed hell-bent on inflicting plagues of frogs and locusts, destroying wicked cities and wreaking mighty tempests rather than in showing compassion.

It was not easy to reconcile his love of man with his insatiable lust for destruction. He was forever on the rampage, condemning unfortunates to years of wandering in deserts, bringing down the walls of cities, smashing tablets and destroying temples because the people would not obey his commands.

As we grew a little older we took all of this less seriously, even mischievously asking questions of a curate who tried to explain the antics of some kind of magician who turned reluctant women into pillars of salt and caused bushes and rods respectively to burst into flame or flower as a conjuror might produce a rabbit from a hat. There was no satisfactory answer. Unless we believed we should not, when the fever of life was over, be granted eternal rest, which seemed to be looking unnecessarily far into the future. At home the reaction was similar. "Who could possibly part an ocean?" I asked. The answer was simple — God. Expressions of such impiety brought immediate castigation for blasphemy. To pursue the topic further was inadvisable. It could only bring the Day of Judgment nearer.

Now Jesus was quite a different character. He was gentle and kind. We didn't know what God looked like. No-one had dared to paint his likeness, but there were plenty of pictures of Jesus, either as a well-formed baby in his mother's arms or as a languid, pale-faced young man with sad eyes. He had long fair hair and Teutonic complexion and features, which seemed odd when he had been born in Bethlehem. Sometimes he was depicted dejectedly surveying the Holy City from a desolate rock, or haloed with eyes upturned towards a host of cherubim and seraphim that circled above, or at other times he was featured in a shepherd's guise leaning on a crook all but engulfed by a flock of sheep or surrounded by angelic-looking infants. You could relate to Jesus. He sat at God's right hand in a house which, paradoxically, had "many mansions". More humane than God, he did not seem intent on destroying what he had created, but occupied himself curing diseases, making the blind see, raising the dead and restoring reckless prodigals to their families.

Sunday afternoon brought no respite. Sunday was Sunday and Sunday School was obligatory until, after almost ten years, I earned parental disapproval by refusing to go.

Mr Wright, the Sunday School Superintendent, and his acolytes, male and female, organised the afternoon's ordeal. It did have the advantage of providing some relief from an otherwise dreary afternoon and a chance to indulge in larking about afterwards with friends who were similarly obligated. The proceedings varied only in the hymns we sang, the lessons, the catechism to be learnt collectively and the verses to be learnt by heart that were assigned to each Sunday and indicated on a card issued to each of us by the Parish Church.

We assembled in the hall to sing *Onward, Christian*

Soldiers or a similar hymn of a more militant nature than the soulful dirges endured at morning service. After the opening prayers and the catechism we were despatched, according to age and sex, to a classroom where, in our case, Mr Matthews, an earnest young man with soulful brown eyes and, for the time, inappropriately long hair, sought to beguile us with that week's lesson. Those of us who had a Bible were commissioned to find, as instructed on the card, *2 Cor.11, v.4-33, Eph.6,v.10* or whatever was appropriate for the occasion. Interpretation and location of these hieroglyphics, either through unfamiliarity or by deliberate intent, could occupy several minutes of fumbling and rustling of pages before we were regaled with miracles of water being turned into wine, walking on water, the multiplying of loaves and fishes to feed thousands, and others that strained credulity beyond reason. Explanations were not easily come by and questions usually dismissed by "You have to believe; otherwise . . ." He never completed the sentence but rolled his compelling eyes upwards and we were left wondering whether he was seeking Divine guidance or expecting the descent of fiery chariots on his incredulous flock.

The Parables were more easily understood. We could appreciate why the wise virgins kept their lamps filled with oil and the stupidity of the foolish ones who neglected to do so, and of the futility of sowing seed on barren ground. There were plenty of analogous examples around us. A "certain man" who was set upon by thieves cropped up regularly, so regularly that we knew by heart that he was going to be robbed of his

91

"raiment", found by a good Samaritan and lodged at an inn for twopence. Twopence, only enough to buy a packet of five Woodbines, and such robbery with violence seemed beyond comprehension but it had all taken place long ago and in some foreign country.

Crime was something we read about in the Sunday newspapers. It did not happen here. There were standards, expectations and obligations. The thrill of a chase — yes. That was irresistible and anyone whose hat was unfortunately sent into a spin by a capricious breeze would have seen half a dozen of us in pursuit to restore it to its owner, but to steal anything, let alone anyone's "raiment", would not have occurred to us. Stealing was wrong. There could be direful consequences. The Holy Trinity — yes, there were three of them — who watched over us, spied on us and threatened terrible retribution. They were known to have inflicted terrible sores on people, thrown them to lions in a pit or into a burning, fiery furnace. We didn't really imagine such things could still happen but miscreants could be punished by birching. Religion could be very frightening but it did instill into us a code of conduct laid down in the Ten Commandments.

A bell summoned us back to the Assembly Hall for final prayers and the singing of *Soldiers of Christ Arise* or a similar one encouraging us to fight the good fight. During the final hymn a collection was taken for the Church Missionary Society. A receipt was issued for each penny given and ten of the receipts could be exchanged for an illustrated text for hanging on the bedroom wall. To inspire us the Church Missionary

Society sometimes sent one of its missionaries, recently returned from "darkest Africa", to talk about his work. Invariably he was greeted by the singing of *From Greenland's Icy Mountains.*

The missionary, either bronzed by sunshine or yellowed by jaundice, would launch into an enlightening account of his conversion of savages who dwelled in heathen lands afar where they brooded in thick darkness bowing down to idols of wood and stone. Thoughts of our pennies had sustained him during his vicissitudes and also, he added with mounting excitement, during encounters with the tigers and snakes that presented him with daily hazards.

It was during a particularly vivid account of an escape from the jaws of a determined crocodile that Mr Matthews, who was standing behind us, revealed an unsuspected sense of humour, by muttering *sotto voce* which was audible to many of us that he wished the crocodile had won. We should, at least, have been spared such a long drawn out report. Fortunately for the speaker the unsuccessful attempts by some of his audience to contain its merriment were construed as admiration of his triumph over a restive reptile. If the idea behind these talks was a hope that some of us might be inspired to become missionaries it was unsuccessful. No-one felt inclined to emulate Doctor Livingstone. A less eventful life in Perry Common seemed preferable to a hazardous one in darkest Africa.

There were some compensations; simple rewards. The religious festivals provided some excitement. Attendance on Palm Sunday was rewarded by the presentation of a palm leaf folded like a crucifix that we could use as a bookmark, but Good Friday was solemnly observed. No-one worked except, of course, wives and mothers. Boiled fish was served at mid-day. The whole duration was supposed to be spent in reflection and contemplation.

By contrast Easter Sunday was a joyous occasion. Everyone put on their best clothes; ostensibly an outward sign of thanks to God but also to impress other churchgoers. For the Harvest Festival we all took offerings of vegetable marrows, potatoes or apples that were displayed around the church. I never knew where they went but there was some satisfaction for having taken part in a tangible thanksgiving. Christmas, and a church decorated with a crib and a Christmas tree, the singing of familiar carols and the exchange of greetings, was the climax of the year.

There were other events, unconnected with the religious festivals. The anniversary of the founding of the Sunday School was honoured with significant pomp as we processed along the estate roads, all the girls dressed in white, led by the Boys' Brigade band. Regular attendance at Sunday School was rewarded by the presentation of a book at the end of year prize giving and being allowed to take part in the annual Sunday School "treat" in the summer. As juniors we were walked to a field in Hawthorn Road to take part in games and races with sweets as prizes and given a picnic tea. Promotion to senior status was rewarded by an outing to the Lickey Hills.

For many it was the only time they were taken beyond

the estate's confines and the weeks immediately preceding the event saw an increase in Sunday School attendance. The outing was undertaken on special trams that left the Short Heath terminus and travelled by a complicated route involving reversals in town because there were no direct cross-city routes.

The return from afternoon Sunday School sometimes found our parents and any visitors attired in their "Sunday best" ready for a walk around Witton Lakes, Perry Park or in the surrounding countryside. There had not, of course, to be any running, jumping, unseemly shouting or anything else likely to contravene the decorum of an English Sunday afternoon.

If there had been a bereavement among the neighbours, a visit to the cemetery became an obligatory substitute. It was not only in the hope of meeting the sorrowing family to offer condolences, but also to admire the floral tributes. Embarrassed and uncomfortable at such encounters, I would detach myself out of earshot of the hushed condolences to feign interest in the stonemasons' craft exemplified in the hosts of recording angels, flying archangels, seraphs and cherubs that adorned the surrounding headstones.

The cemetery was thronged on Sunday afternoons. Visits by the recently-bereaved were called for; a self-imposed ritual that continued for weeks, sometimes for years after the interment. Cremation was not considered as an acceptable alternative to burial. The morbidly curious also walked in the cemetery for the sole purpose of inspecting the headstones, reading the epitaphs and admiring the blossoms displayed in the ornamental urns.

The Victorians' obsession with death hung on during the first thirty years of the century, and the stonemasons and florists flourished on the eccentricities of grieving relatives by providing suitable, and often exotic, memorials and tributes to those who were "not dead but gone before".

Cemetery-going was so much in vogue that special buses were run to the cemetery gates on Sunday afternoons, and those who had omitted to buy their flowers beforehand were able to do so from the flower sellers who had arrived by earlier buses in anticipation of unloading the blooms they had been unable to dispose of on Saturday.

After a couple of years and having established both church and Sunday school, the Reverend Harris left and was replaced by the Reverend Cooke of short and rotund stature. He was a vivacious character with a rubicund complexion who enlivened the church services we were forced to attend. His enthusiasm for social activities had to be curbed by the lack of a church hall. Singing and dancing could not be indulged in within the church and it was not until 1932 that a wooden church hall was erected.

Mr Cooke made a habit of dropping in at our home and got on well with my father, which was surprising as his faith in religion had all but been destroyed during the Great War, but he found in the Reverend Cooke a mutual interest in bell ringing. On one occasion we even heard him exclaim "He's quite good as clergymen go" and, as good clergymen, like good cooks, go, Mr Cooke went. Saint Martin's was never more than a curacy where incumbents rarely stayed for more than a few years. His replacement was a solemn young man of God, whose saturnine appearance and tongue-tied embarrassment at meeting parishioners in the road was only overcome when he climbed into his pulpit. The transformation was dramatic. He became excited, tying and untying his stole as he harangued us on the iniquities of the world around us, of its perils and vicissitudes, our own wickedness and temptations. Our reactions of ill-stifled laughter did not accord with his expectations and only served to spur him on to greater efforts as he challenged us from his pulpit like Elijah provoking the priests of Baal from Mount Carmel. His was not the church militant; it was the church violent and, had we been anywhere but in church, I am sure we should have given him a round of applause.

It was not until the Sunday Cinema Bill was passed in 1932, and not without opposition, that there was any leavening of a depressing day. Our Mother condemned Sunday cinema-going. "There are plenty of days to go to the cinema without spoiling Sundays," she said resentfully, even though the films that were shown were considered to be appropriate for the Sabbath. The cinemas that did open their doors on Sundays did much to relieve the gloom of days that were only enlightened by the thought of more nourishing food than that served during the rest of the week. It occurred to no-one to be absent from the traditional Sunday lunch.

It was the family meal of the week, although simple by today's expectations. It was the only one at which a joint of meat was served. This was invariably beef, pork or lamb, according to the season, and for which the equivalent of 25p was budgeted. It was served with roast potatoes and one other vegetable. Poultry was a rarity. A chicken was bought in its plumage and had to be plucked, singed and trussed. A process that took a whole evening and festooned the kitchen with feathers. Wine was out of the question. It was much too expensive and not to be encouraged, but sometimes a bottle of home-made ginger beer would be opened. A rice pudding cooked, for reasons of economy, in the same oven and at the same time as the joint of meat, followed. Sunday tea was also traditional. Tinned salmon and salad, followed by tinned fruit and a home-made fruit cake was the usual fare. Sons and daughters who were "walking out" with girl or boy friends could be excused provided that they were eating at the homes of the intended spouse.

Food, and sometimes the dispensing of a pennyworth of sweets by a visiting aunt, were the only treats until we were teenagers. Sunday was a day of preaching and teaching, discipline and discomfort. It was a different day in a different world and it was only fear of the unknown that prevented many of us from becoming defiant infidels.

The Black Country
Connection

Family ancestry imposed obligations for ritual visits to relatives in the Black Country. As we rarely travelled beyond the city's confines and only had a seaside holiday once a year, these visits were exciting events eagerly anticipated.

To many who lived within the city's boundaries the Black Country was remote and unexplored; a region where the customs, habits and ceremonies of a people who spoke with an unfamiliar dialect, were different from their own. There was little communication between the two and they were distanced from each other beyond the city's western limits by open country, much of it despoiled by subsidence, pit mounds and the derelict workings of coal mines; a wasteland crossed only by canals, railways and the undulating tracks of the two tramway companies that had succeeded in penetrating Birmingham territory.

Beyond this no-man's land lay the towns of the Black Country, all fussily independent, their inhabitants cautious, suspicious, hostile even towards their neighbours. Dudley folk could be very distrustful of "them from Bilston" and confrontation at boundaries was not unusual. A steam roller once placed across the tram tracks by Handsworth had been a display of force and a deliberate attempt to provoke a "border incident" by preventing trams from West Bromwich from entering its territory. Smethwick alone was physically joined to the city by continuous housing. Its inhabitants, maintaining that they were neither of Birmingham nor the Black Country but Staffordshire, had elected to remain citizens of a non-aligned county borough; a kind of buffer state between Birmingham and the Black Country proper. Consequently the boundary along the city's western side assumed a position second only to that of a national frontier, or so it seemed to us as children.

No corporation vehicle ever crossed into another's territory, with the unfortunate result that Birmingham's bus routes Numbers 6 and 7 were forced to terminate at Sandon and Portland Roads respectively and at some distance from natural changing points just across the boundary in Smethwick, and no West Bromwich corporation buses breached the boundary at the Hawthorns. Only the trams were allowed to cross, their passengers subjected to a curious ritual because tickets were not issued at the point of embarkation for journeys in either direction across the boundary where the tram came to a halt and the conductor solemnly called "Boundary," which precipitated a vexed fumbling in pockets and handbags for coins as he collected fares anew and issued fresh tickets.

An even more curious ceremony had only recently been abandoned. Birmingham had objected to the bamboo rod carried on the Black Country trams for turning the trolley pole and insisted that this be changed at the boundary for the trolley rope favoured by the city. On the return journey the procedure was reversed.

Visits to relatives in Smethwick were usually accomplished by tram from the terminus behind the Council House and approached via Eden Place, reputed to be the draughtiest passage in the city. The trams on this route were, until 1928, run, not by the corporation, but by the Birmingham District Power and Traction Company, whose impressive title was not reflected in its antiquated vehicles. The trams were badly maintained and made sounds quite different from those of the corporation, especially when travelling along the ill-worn tracks outside the city. They shuddered and shook as they ground up the long steep incline of Cape Hill; wooden coachwork creaking and windows rattling at every rail joint. It was an endurance test for the ageing vehicles that sighed with relief as they surmounted the brow of the hill and the tone of the overheating motors regained composure.

Expeditions beyond Smethwick were invariably made by train, because such bus routes as there were were circuitous, the buses infrequent and unreliable, and progress by tram was slow. A journey from Perry Common to Dudley, now taking but a few minutes by motorway, could occupy a couple of hours and be complicated by several changes and long waits. These outings involved a great deal of preparation, discussion and speculation over the route to be taken to ensure that the maximum advantages of time and economy in fares could be gained.

Excitement intensified at the prospect of a railway

journey. It had been as recently as 1923 that over a hundred railway companies had been amalgamated into the "Big Four" that survived until nationalisation, but it was many years before the engines and pre-war rolling stock were replaced or re-painted in their new colours. Consequently we never knew what we were likely to travel in until the train arrived but, before such eventualities, there were preparations to be made.

A postcard announcing the intended visit would be despatched at least a week before giving details of the route anticipated and the expected time of arrival. The first part of the journey was to town on a Number 5 bus, burdened with bags containing the customary fruit cake as an offering in one and spare clothing in case of accidents, such as tearing one's trousers or falling into a pond, in another. Whichever route was chosen we usually found ourselves deposited beneath the vast glass canopy of Snow Hill's magnificent booking hall while tickets were being purchased at one of the little windows, some marked "First" and others "Third", each surmounted by a pointed architrave, that stood along a marble-faced wall like a row of sentry boxes, and each with a tiny opening through which a ticket clerk peeped.

A wooden barrier, polished over the years by thousands of waiting elbows, prevented more than one person at a time approaching him. Watching other people operating a tall red platform ticket machine was a diversion during the waiting time. The machine had a narrow glass panel in its front through which we could see a stack of cardboard tickets. An inserted penny clattered through a mechanical labyrinth and dropped into a metal drawer. The purchaser pulled a shiny brass handle and a ticket was delivered.

The railway tickets obtained, we ran ahead to the concourse where a man stood at a sliding gate ready to punch the tickets before letting us pass. The whole splendour of the station lay below and could be taken in at a glance as we descended the wide staircase. It was ecstasy to take in the panorama displayed in the bustle, colour, noise and smell of the trains; steam escaping from engine cylinders, smoke being puffed towards the glass roof, whistles impatiently shrieking and goods trains trundling slowly through on the platform-avoiding lines. Snow Hill was rarely quiet and, because its platforms were so long, trains did not slide gently into the main line platforms they burst spectacularly out of the tunnel with dramatic splendour, a full head of steam and a quarter of a mile of platform ahead.

As plenty of time was always allowed there was ample in which to examine the fascinating machines that stood along Platform 5. At one of them a bar of chocolate could be dispensed with a penny, at another a card with one's weight printed on it, but, most intriguing of all, was the one where you could spell out your name on a metal strip by moving a clock-like hand to successive letters and pulling a lever to emboss them. There were no disturbing loudspeaker announcements for train departures so we had to watch a porter at a wooden finger post who slotted into position arms bearing the destinations of departing trains and a pointing finger to direct travellers to the correct platform. The arms not being used were stored in a box at the base of the finger post.

The biggest thrill was to travel on the Birkenhead Express as far as Wolverhampton. This was not very often, but it was here on Platform 5 that Great Aunt Alice caused consternation and apprehension among her relatives one Saturday afternoon in 1930.

Aunt Alice was my mother's aunt; a legendary figure known only to us through her letters. She had long ago left her native soil and married a man in Manchester. When he died she became housekeeper to a cleric in a remote Devon village. There she married again. This time a local man who claimed never to have seen a railway train. He was quite satisfied with the local carrier's horse and cart which took him and Aunt Alice to the nearest town once a week.

It was soon after his death that Aunt Alice elected to visit her Black Country relatives, proposing to stay with each for a few days. "Shall arrive by the afternoon train," she had written. Her information was confirmed by consulting timetables, and we assembled with other relatives on Number 5 Platform to meet the afternoon train from the West Country. The train roared in. There was a fluster of activity as passengers descended. The train went on its way and the platform cleared but there was no sign of Aunt Alice.

The immediate reaction was one of concern. Had Aunt Alice, now fairly advanced in years, been carried on to Wolverhampton, missed her train or met with unforeseen circumstances? There was no way of finding out and, after exhausting all possibilities, the welcoming party returned to New Street Station to catch the next train to Tipton to report Aunt Alice's non-arrival to her sister, Great Aunt Ebrina, who awaited her appearance with her escort of nephews and nieces.

Arrival at the Tipton home found Great Aunt Alice, a diminutive figure dressed sombrely in black with her hair drawn tightly back into a bun at the nape of her neck, ensconced on a dining chair ("I never sit in an armchair," she later declared when staying with us, "such being bad for the posture"). She demanded imperiously to know where those who had been deputed to meet her in Birmingham had been. "I waited at New Street Station for half an hour before catching the local train to Tipton." "At New Street!," said her astounded nephew, Uncle Fred. "We were at Snow Hill to meet the Exeter train of course. What were you doing at New Street? We naturally assumed . . ." She didn't give him time to finish. "You might assume — I reason, and I reasoned that if I had stayed on the train from Exeter to Snow Hill, my luggage would have been a nuisance to carry to New Street for my connection to Tipton. Now, by changing from the Great Western to the Midland at Bristol it was so much easier."

"But Aunt you didn't tell us your intention. You haven't been for years. You might have got lost or . . ." "Got lost!," retorted Aunt Alice with tremendous dignity. "Do you think I don't know my way around Birmingham?" and turning to Uncle Fred she concluded the episode with "Now, young man, you can go down to Tipton Station and fetch my luggage."

Aunt Alice was only one of the many people to have

been met or seen off from Platform 5, but it was more usual to be dragged reluctantly away from the fascinating machines to the bay platforms where the local trains stood with impatiently hissing engines. These were usually drawn by Prairie or Pannier tank engines with a train of old compartment-type stock, lit by gas and with faded sepia photographs depicting resorts served by the railway displayed above the seats and below a netted luggage rack. Under the window hung a heavy leather strap that could be pulled to raise or lower the window. It was accepted that the passenger occupying the seat next to the window and facing the direction of travel had control of this. Consequently this was the seat we coveted so that we could operate the window whenever the engine driver's whistle warned of the approach to a tunnel when it was very necessary to close all the windows to prevent the intrusion of smoke and smuts from the engine.

The actual journeys were far more exciting than the purpose of the visits where you were expected to be on best behaviour, and any time waiting for connections at junctions was whiled away watching the movement of signals, points and trucks being shunted. The waiting rooms at the Black Country stations were lofty and depressing, and sparsely furnished with horsehair-upholstered benches that prickled the backs of short-trousered legs. A solid, heavy and immovable table occupied the middle of the room. I never saw it used. It was situated at an inconvenient distance from the benches arranged along the walls decorated with dis-coloured and peeling posters. In winter groups of passengers stood huddled around a bright fire, replenished periodically by a porter, that burned in a grate situated at a distance from the table and benches which no-one attempted to move any nearer.

Many of our excursions were to Netherton on the western side of Dudley, where my Mother was born, and the last stages of the journey were undertaken on a Black Country tramcar from Dudley Market Place. It was an exhilarating but frightening experience. By 1930 the whole of the Black Country tramways had become so dilapidated that it was derided and ridiculed. The trams were antiquated and mining subsidence had reduced the tracks to a fearful condition in some places and caused the standards that supported the overhead wires to lean drunkenly out of perpendicular. It was all in stark contrast to the Birmingham system whose trams were immaculately maintained and the trackwork kept in flawless condition. Within a short time, and except for the two routes into Birmingham, the trams had gone, replaced by Midland "Red" buses or trolleybuses. The overhead wires were dismantled, but the trackwork and standards, like monumental columns, remained for years.

It was a point of honour that visitors be met at the final point of disembarkation. There were bags and umbrellas to be carried and solicitous enquiries concerning the rigours of the journey to be made. It was during the last stages of the journey that my mother always changed her gloves, soiled by the smoke and dirt of the excursion. It was all part of a ritual. "No-one ever arrives in soiled gloves," she told us. There were so many reminders of what was done and what was not done that it was difficult to keep abreast of what was expected. A mistake was inevitably followed by an admonition that "A gentleman never . . ." if you failed to raise your cap, stand up when a lady entered a room or hesitated to give up your seat to a lady in a crowded tramcar.

Upon arrival at the final destination, the divesting of outer garments occupied considerable time and was punctuated and delayed by animated conversation concerning the health and welfare of those present and extended to those not present. These preliminaries had to be endured with patience. There were, in order of precedence, hats and hatpins to be removed and the pins repositioned, gloves to be carefully peeled off and pressed flat, coats to be taken off, smoothed and hung behind the door of some dark recess. In winter the time was increased by the divesting of gaiters, scarves and a layer of flannel worn beneath coats as a "chest protector". Such impedimenta, ludicrous as they may seem, were considered very necessary when journeys were undertaken in unheated public transport and involved long waits on draughty stations or in drenching storms at exposed tram stops.

All the Black Country homes we visited were similar, but varied from those in Birmingham in that the kitchen, or "brewus" (brew house) as it was usually called, was separated from the main building. It was something to do with fire regulations, I think, or to prevent unwelcome smells from pervading the rest of the house. A front parlour, rarely used, opened directly onto the street. Some had a paved area in lieu of a front garden. This was referred to as the "fode". The front door was only used for three occasions; weddings and funerals, to permit the egress of brides and coffins respectively, and for visits by the doctor who, by virtue of his status, was accorded this privilege. All others gained admission via the entry between the houses to the back door and the living room.

Preparations for the mid-day meal, which had been put well in hand earlier, were hastened with renewed vigour as the womenfolk disappeared to the "brewus" leaving us to be entertained by exploits devised by younger members of the family.

The mid-day meal consumed, there was a brief pause while the grown-ups revitalised themselves with cups of tea before embarking on a tight afternoon schedule calling on other relatives and friends in the locality. The walks between them being interrupted at appropriate places by indications of a grave where the relics of a departed relative lay, a colliery at which someone had met an untimely end, and the schools and churches attended, each punctuated by a homily which left an impression that previous generations had had little to rejoice over. Their lives seemed to have been constant battles against starvation, sickness and poverty, death and a constant fear of imminent destruction, either by the elements, illness or the result of mining accidents.

The startling effects of mining subsidence were evident in many dwellings, some of them had sunk several feet on their foundations, or leaned perilously out of perpendicular and had pit props supporting them to prevent complete collapse.

A welcome relief from those homes where we were expected to be seen but not heard occurred if the way lay past Netherton Ironworks or Hingley's where, courtesy of people known to us, we were allowed inside to watch the molten metal pouring from furnaces to be puddled and run into moulds or emerging from between rollers to be handled by men stripped to the waist because of the intense heat. These were impressive sights which, we were told, had built Britain's prosperity. It seemed a hollow word. Few who worked there appeared to share in that prosperity yet I never heard any complaints. It was all placidly accepted as an inevitable way of life.

The late nineteenth century, of which we were constantly reminded, lay beyond my memory, yet its proximity was made vivid by great aunts born in mid-century who recalled with great clarity events of their own youth. Born before the Education Act of 1870 such education they had received had been at a "Dame's School" at a cost of one penny a week but, before going to school, they had risen at five o'clock each day to go out to collect cinders and bits of coal from pit banks to light a fire to boil a kettle to make tea for their menfolk before some of them set off on a five-mile walk to work. The privations, desperation and determination of such folk had made them literate, numerate and shrewd. Their early lives made ours, even in the depressed thirties, seem Elysian.

The courtesy visits ended, a sumptuous Black Country tea could be looked forward to. Cold meat, salad, pickled onions and plenty of bread and butter and cake were traditional fare. The clearing up accomplished, preparations for the return journey were begun. Tradition demanded that departing guests were accompanied to the point of departure to be properly "seen off". Ample time was allowed with the result that there were several minutes to be whiled away at tram stop or station. All tongues having been thoroughly exercised during the day most topics had been exhausted and, with little time in which to begin new ones, the waiting time was one of uneasy silence broken by platitudes: "Come again soon," "Mind how you go," "Don't forget you have to change at," etc. The ringing of a signal box bell or the appearance of a tram on the horizon was a sign for renewed thanks, farewells and exhortations to "take care".

In the Black Country life went at a slower pace than in Birmingham and trams and buses rarely started before everyone was seated. There was, as a result, plenty of time for smiling, waving and mouthing through the windows. It was not unknown in that easy-going atmosphere for the conductor to be asked to stop the tram because "I forgot to ask about Cousin Maud."

As the glow of the blast furnaces faded in the darkening skies and was replaced by the bright street lights of Birmingham there was time to reflect on the differences of life in the Black Country. Whether the visits were to Aunt Keziah, Aunt Sarah or Great Aunt Ebrina in Dudley or to the three spinsters, Harriet, Ada and Maud (whose very names evoke the age in which they lived) in Smethwick, we were overwhelmed with unfeigned affection like returned prodigals as, in Black Country terminology, they would "bring the pantry out."

Only in the Black Country Museum, where it is possible to ride on a tram and see inside the preserved houses and shops, can the atmosphere of a vanished way of life be recaptured.

Depression and Despondency 1929-

All winters at Perry Common were hard. Its high altitude made it especially vulnerable and the inhabitants had good reason for rechristening it "perishing Common" in 1929 when unremitting snow fell for several days. It was one of the most severe winters in Europe ever recorded. It was bitterly cold and an angry wind swept across from the Bleak Hills whistling the snow into deep drifts along the road which quickly became blocked, frustrating the delivery men whose frosted-breath horses slipped and slithered on the ice.

A hard frost set in and the unfreezing of pipes and cisterns which froze afresh each night in our poorly-heated homes was added to the daily routine. Indoors it needed some courage to leave the fireside, and errands to other parts of the house were delayed as long as possible. Upstairs, opening the door to a bedroom was like opening a refrigerator. A chill struck back from the bedroom walls and furniture. Ice patterns covered the window panes and you returned from the outside lavatory with chattering teeth and frozen fingers.

No buses appeared and getting to work presented problems, but not to have gone would have resulted in worse ones; an inevitable loss in wages. My father, his lower limbs encased in a pair of leather leggings, set out

113

each morning to walk through snow that was, in some places, up to his knees. The clearing of snow from frontages was left to womenfolk, children and shopkeepers. With the poor tools available it was an exerting task, but the dilemma for adults was a delight for children.

Thick ice formed over Witton Lakes. No-one could remember a time when they had frozen so completely that the ice around the edges was broken and they were declared safe enough to venture upon. The word spread quickly and it seemed that the whole population turned out one memorable weekend to enjoy the free entertainment provided by nature. The intrepid to sample the delights of walking and sliding upon the ice, the timid to line the banks to cheer or jeer at their attempts. My mother unearthed a pair of skates she had bought in her youth and surprised us with her dexterity. We made a toboggan and dragged it to the lakes to join those of others hastily constructed from wooden crates scrounged from the greengrocer. On the banks, punctured cans filled with glowing cinders were swung by the spectators to keep the fuel alive to warm the hands of those who fell.

It was some time before a thaw relieved the misfortunes of the grown-ups and threatened for us the joys of revelry at a time when there was little to rejoice over. Suddenly the Wall Street crash sparked off the biggest depression the world had ever known, and the bleak winter was followed by a chill of a different kind as men were laid off work or put on short time and the promising sunrise began to fade like a mirage in the desert. At first, and because of the variety of its industry, Birmingham was not so badly hit as some of the northern towns and South Wales, and the city was invaded by men who spoke with unfamiliar accents seeking work in the motor industry that was growing now that the possession of a car was becoming a possibility for some middle class families. Finding lodgings was easy in the homes of those who had lost their jobs with only the faintest hope of finding employment in their own trades although some were successful in the motor and construction industries that continued to thrive.

By eavesdropping from the kitchen on conversations of the committee members of the Women's Co-operative Guild that sometimes met in our living room it was apparent that there was dissatisfaction with successive governments that had been unable to solve the problems of depressions, strikes and lockouts that had bedevilled the country since the end of the war. Names, Ramsay MacDonald, a Mr Snowden and someone whose name sounded like *Lord* George cropped up in conversations and were blamed for not keeping promises they had made.

It was all very confusing. We were well-fed, clothed and, by the standards of the era, comfortable, yet, it seemed, there were thousands still awaiting the homes they had been promised and many were so poor that they could not afford a pair of boots. As with all generations people yearned for "the old days" and the talk always came round to blaming a war of which we knew little but saw reminders everywhere around us. All over the city there were pavement artists in tattered army greatcoats, ramshackle bands, disabled trios and legless ex-servicemen propelling themselves along on boards that had been equipped with little wheels.

Few people understood the reasons for booms and slumps but all were acutely conscious of prices rising as wages went down. We knew very little about the politicians except what we read in the newspapers. How could we? There was no other way then. We couldn't see or hear them. They were unassailable in their ivory towers and as remote from the working classes as the Eskimaux in Greenland but, with an enduring class system unimaginable today, and one where women continued to play a subservient role of cleaning, cooking, washing and ironing; their only relaxation seemed to be that of counting the "dropped stitches" in their knitting, most of them, if not content, were resigned to let what were called the ruling classes rule, but there was a stirring among the more enlightened, especially the women who were not eligible to vote. Many of them were well into their thirties and irked by the stings of injustice in a male-dominated society.

The approach of a general election provoked excited talk and it was obvious from adult conversations that it would be of tremendous significance. Now for the first time women would have equal voting rights with men at twenty-one. The election was to go down in history as the "Flapper" election ("Flapper" was the word in vogue for a flighty young female). Our mother explained how important it was for the women to use their newly-acquired power and that any who failed to do so would be betraying those brave women who had struggled for it over many years.

It was something to do with a Mrs Pankhurst, she said, who had gone around smashing shop windows, another who threw herself under a horse at the Derby, and others who chained themselves to railings in their fight to get voting rights. These seemed strange things for respectable ladies to indulge in but there was no doubt that they had been admired for their efforts, and our mother was vehement in her condemnation of anyone who proposed not to use the privilege won for them by such determined women.

Polling day arrived and so did a policeman, his neck encircled by a mandarin collar of the contemporary uniform, his helmet crowned with a silver spike that gave him another six inches of authority. He stationed himself outside the polling station in the school opposite, presumably to ensure that there were no disturbances. During the day the children banded together according to the persuasions of their parents to indulge in the simple enjoyment of marching along the estate roads waving banners and singing an inane rhyme to the tune of "Tramp, tramp, tramp the boys are marching"

> Vote, vote, vote for Mr —
> He is sure to win the day.
> For we'll get a salmon tin
> And we'll put ole — in
> And he won't go voting anymore.

There were mock battles when we met rival marchers with the object of capturing their banners but little harm was done. Most of us had been friends on the previous

117

day and would be the day after. These harmless escapades provided diversions from the usual daily uneventful routine for participants and spectators alike. The events of that evening are long remembered. It was warm, the windows were open and the noise from the road outside the polling station was too disturbing for sleep. I crept into the front bedroom to witness unprecedented excitement. A crowd had gathered. Those who had voted remained to chat to and encourage those arriving. From the distance came the sound of singing. It was some kind of revolutionary song that the co-operators sometimes sang at their meetings:-

> Men of England, wherefore plough
> For the lords who lay ye low?

The singers rounded the corner from Witton Lodge Road and, although there may not have been many, together with those already assembled, they seemed to fill the road. Someone raised a red flag. A man climbed the school railings and everyone cheered. More banners were raised and the man began to sing:-

> The people's flag is deepest red,
> It shrouded oft our martyr'd dead,
> And ere their limbs grew stiff and cold,
> Their heart's blood dyed its ev'ry fold

The haunting words made a disturbing impression on a young mind. More people joined in the singing:

Raise the scarlet banner high.
Within its shade we'll live and die.
Though cowards flinch and traitors sneer,
We'll keep the red flag flying here.

It was sung again and again until I knew all the words. The policeman looked on in a detached kind of way. There was no unseemly behaviour and I never knew how it ended. I was discovered at my listening post and despatched to my bedroom.

The noise continued, and in the imagination of a lively youngster I conjured up visions of revolutions read about in lurid tales. I confidently expected to wake up next day to find the country was in the grip of one. It would be a terrible thing. It wouldn't affect us of course, and it didn't. Next morning the crowds had gone, the policeman had disappeared, there was no singing and everything was back to normal.

A Labour victory, even though it was by a small majority, brought undisguised elation. Now things must change. Everyone was saying that it had been the women's newly-acquired votes that had brought about the result. There was even more rejoicing when, for the first time a woman became a cabinet minister. Miss Margaret Bondfield became Minister of Labour, but the sceptics scoffed "They'll be wanting a woman Prime Minister next."

For the first few months unemployment decreased, but it was a false dawn and, by the end of 1930 it had risen again to a staggering two and a half million. This was far more serious than any subsequent depression because

119

few married women worked and, in most cases, the men were the only breadwinners. There was also a fundamental difference in conditions. There were no social security arrangements or credit facilities. Rents were collected weekly and gas and electricity were paid for as they were used by putting money into slot meters.

Some of the unemployed joined the ranks of the war wounded in the city's streets to sing or unashamedly beg, but most of them had a strong aversion to any form of public relief and would have preferred to work at anything rather than seek aid.

There was no shortage of opinions and suggestions for action, but little was done to initiate anything in the form of work schemes. Imports from Germany of cheap tin toys as part of war reparations only succeeded in reducing the country's own output, and once more the cry went up "It's all because of the war." Peaceful unemployed marchers advanced on London from the dockyards, mills and mines demanding action. They aroused sympathy everywhere and before long there was undisguised condemnation of a government that seemed as powerless as any other since the war to cure the malaise.

The cost of paying unemployment benefit became uncontrollable and a contributory factor in a crisis from which a coalition government emerged. Ramsay MacDonald remained as Prime Minister of a government that increased taxation, reduced wages and abandoned the Gold Standard. The bitterest cuts were those made in unemployment benefit. There were promises that prices would fall but only after wages had been reduced. Little

Union Jacks appeared on home-produced goods to encourage us to "Buy British" but few had any money to buy anything other than the barest essentials. There was no choice but to accept the situation.

Fortunately my father remained in full employment throughout the whole period but all around we saw the distressing effects of the depression at its worst and, with the ever-present threat hovering, economies, ridiculous as they may seem, were made at home. The electric light was only used in the living room. An oil lamp, an heirloom that would command a fair price today, was kept burning on a low flame in the scullery and a "Kelly lamp" burned on a bracket on the landing and was carried from room to room as required. The hot water bottles were replaced by the cast iron shelves taken from the fireside oven and wrapped in newspaper to warm the beds. A mixture of soot and salt was substituted for toothpaste. Clothes were patched and darned and collars and cuffs turned to extend their lives.

There were, doubtless, other economies from which my brother and I were protected. Every penny was considered and any that accumulated were put into the Municipal Bank to earn a little interest. Other people were not so fortunate. Not everyone had been able to save anything to fall back on and many of our friends and neighbours were subjected to the harsh scrutiny of the Means Test Inspector who was usually a young, untrained and unsympathetic member of a team taken on by the new bureaucracy to decide whether or not people qualified to receive any benefit from the state. It was the most degrading system ever introduced by any govern-

121

ment. Clocks, furniture and ornaments were ordered to be sold before any benefit could be considered. As few were in a position to buy the whole situation became ludicrously cruel.

Women who could find work washing, ironing or cleaning grasped the opportunity. Many trudging as far as the wealthier homes in Sutton Coldfield to earn half-a-crown (12p) for a morning's work. Children were sent out with buckets and shovels to prowl after horses to collect their droppings in the hope of selling them as garden manure at a penny a bucket.

Mr Murgatroyd was thrown out of work by the Metropolitan Carriage Company (the "Met" as it was called locally) where he had worked as a carpenter. Our neighbour supplemented his bare income by carving animals and birds from pieces of wood he scrounged. We have one still and I can never look at it without being reminded of the appalling conditions endured and survived. He reached the stage when he was forced to apply for relief from the Public Assistance Department and, in anticipation of the dreaded visit from the Means Test Inspector, the family was already sleeping out the two eldest children at a neighbour's house.

The practice of "sleeping out" by older wage-earning children was widely used as a way round the Means Test which took account of the number of wage earners in a family who could be expected to contribute towards its maintenance. The "sleepers-out" left home in the late evening and returned at breakfast time next day. They could, as a result, be declared as non-domiciled. There was no shortage of beds among the neighbours who were glad enough to provide a service for a few coppers a night. The Means Test Inspector was regarded as fair game, and desperate situations demanded desperate remedies.

Mrs Murgatroyd called over the garden fence with her customary cup of tea after the mid-day meal to recount the inspector's visit. "He looked at all the furniture and told us what we ought to sell," she said. "Then he counted the sheets and looked at the coats hanging in the hall. Asked if we had any relatives who could help and —," she laughed derisively, "wanted to see our savings books." As with others in her situation the best food was reserved for her husband. She often went without, telling him she had already eaten. "All I've had today," she confided, "is a few cups of tea and a bit of bread and lard." An outward sign of impoverishment was an oil lamp on the living room table; a sign that there was no money to put in the electric light meter.

There were many times my mother would bake extra and offer the surplus to our neighbours on the pretext that she had baked too much. She was too methodical by far ever to have baked more than was needed but her offerings were gratefully received. She knew what she was doing and so did the neighbours, but dignity had been upheld through diplomacy.

By listening to adult conversations it became apparent that the new world for which the war had been fought remained out of reach. People had been led to believe that the post-war world would be a better place and that the defeated Germans would pay for this, but how could they when we understood that their plight was worse than ours? There was no way the world could be a better place. It had to be worse. Expectations beyond all hope of fulfilment had been raised during the war, but such was the naivety of thought that it was not until the depression that people began to realise just how much they had been misled by propaganda. They began to blame the politicians. It was Lloyd George's fault, or Ramsay MacDonald's. The hopes of earlier years turned sour. Disillusion and cynicism became the prevailing moods. The dreams of the returned soldiers for whom nothing would be too good, turned into nightmares, and a population that had been led to expect everything now looked forward to nothing.

There were many attempts by altruistic societies, institutions and individuals to alleviate the hardships. The Lord Mayor launched a distress fund and an illuminated tramcar toured the city in support of his appeal. The *Birmingham Mail*, concerned over the plight of children at Christmas, launched a Christmas tree fund so that no child should be without a Christmas tree. It was so successful that it was followed up by a "Coal for Christmas" campaign. The owners of the *Daily Mail*, ostensibly moved by the sight of poorly-clad children, began a scheme whereby readers who collected a specified quantity of serial numbers cut from the front page of the paper could obtain a pair of children's boots. The scheme was more likely to have been an attempt to keep up the circulation at a time when there were many who could not afford to buy a paper. The *Daily Mail* boots, as they were quick to be called, were crude, clumsy and so heavily studded with hob nails and steel tips that half a dozen children wearing them and running along the road sounded like a cavalry charge.

The boots were so obvious that anyone wearing a pair became an object of thoughtless ridicule, and none can be more malevolent than children in inflicting mental torture on those less fortunate than they are. I saw many unfortunate children, some of them girls, wearing such boots, often without the comfort of a pair of socks. The insensitive jeering they endured must have left an indelible impression.

There were other newspapers also concerned over diminishing circulations, that introduced insurance schemes, free gifts and offers to fill shelves with cheap editions of the classics at reduced prices. These schemes had the advantage of decreasing the number of unemployed who were only too willing to become canvassers for £3.00 a week to knock on doors with a line of sales patter extolling the virtues of a particular newspaper. Housewives were assailed daily by university graduates trying to sell commodities which few wanted or could afford. It was, however, through the persistence of a determined salesman that we acquired an eight-volume set of *Cassell's Book of Knowledge*, an encyclopaedia that provided hours of enjoyment and fruitful learning.

The Co-operative Women's Guild continued to meet in the school opposite every Wednesday evening. Many of its members had been reduced to tragic circumstances; those who had been poor were becoming impoverished, but an evening out at the Guild gave them an opportunity to share their troubles, and there was a sad irony when they rose to:-

Sing of the glorious coming day
When want and care shall pass away,
And men with truth and willing mind
A new and better world shall find.

Our mother sometimes "discovered" clothes that we had outgrown and tactfully offered them as "being useful for patching". They were rarely used as such but worn by other children as received. We were encouraged to give away some of our toys to those who had none. The *Evening Despatch*, long since absorbed into the *Birmingham Evening Mail*, ran a children's club which they called the "Nig Nogs", a name that would scarcely be welcomed today. A subscription of one shilling entitled you to a badge and sundry literature. Members were encouraged to form local groups to raise funds. An effort at carol singing raised eleven shillings (55p) and a magic lantern show in our home and given on our Victorian magic lantern raised half-a-crown. Thirty children who had paid a penny each were crammed into the living room where my father operated the lantern and my mother gave a commentary on the slides. Coffee and biscuits were provided in the interval.

The appalling conditions endured during the depression raised a generation that learned to stand on its own feet and make its own decisions. If it didn't there was no-one else who would. There was apathy but the conditions were accepted without much protest. There were a few vocal protests but they achieved little. The unemployed and their families were far too busy trying to supplement their meagre incomes by chopping firewood they hoped to sell, digging their gardens and sieving ashes to retrieve a few cinders to ignite a fire. Memories of the failure of the General Strike were still bitter, but it occurred to no-one to defy the law. The men who were employed worked hard and did not query what they had to do because there was an ever-present threat of being "laid off", and outside the factory gates was a queue of men eager to take their jobs.

There were other more deeply-rooted reasons why there were so few protests. The generation that reached maturity in the 1930s had been brought up to rely on itself. It may not have been very well educated; many had left school at ten years of age, but it had been conditioned and disciplined to do as it was told and not to question authority. Most people were too proud to ask for help. There was a stigma attached to "supping on others" end, incredible as it may seem, there was an ever-present dread of the workhouse, especially among the elderly, for it was only in 1929 that those dreaded institutions had been abolished in the city and responsibility for the destitute transferred to the local authority.

Overlooking Perry Common and dominating the skyline at the summit of Reservoir Road the grim forbidding silhouette of the old workhouse (now Highcroft Hospital) stood out; a landmark for miles around and a reminder that times had been worse in the closing years of the previous century. Conditions were no worse than many had been brought up to expect, and a patient resignation prevailed; the product of long histories of deprivation and suffering, of poverty and tragedy. There were many whose outlook seemed to have reached the depths of pessimism who came to seek our mother's advice and comfort. They were rarely disappointed.

The politicians had promised that things would improve, that better times were on the horizon and that they believed the corner had been turned. Few believed them. Too many promises had not been fulfilled. The Promised Land was always in sight but the people, like those of Moses, seemed doomed never to enter it. The songs of the era *Buddy, can you spare a Dime?*, *Underneath the Arches*, *Stormy Weather* and others drawled over the air by the crooners reflected the lassitude of the age, and even *Blaze Away* did little to assuage anyone's feelings, while the *Stein Song*, with its stirring tune and words:-

> Drink to all the happy days
> To the careless hours

. . . served only to recall for our parents' generation nostalgia for the idyllic Edwardian days of their youth, but then "all times when old are good".

Despite the depressing situation, some amelioration, sparse though it was, was provided by national, municipal and voluntary organisations in a way that would have been undreamed of a few years earlier. Old people and widows received pensions of ten shillings (50p) a week and there were free dinners for deprived children. The welfare state was a long way off but no-one needed to fear starvation or the workhouse.

"Gotta Cigarette Card, Mister?"

"Gotta cigarette card, mister?" clamoured a clutch of little boys who besieged the buses disgorging the returning workers at the Circle terminus each evening.

Sometimes their appeals bore fruit, but the men jumping off the buses before they had come to a standstill were in a hurry to get home and were likely to have children of their own who collected the treasured cards. Making collections of almost anything; tram and bus tickets, transfers, matchbox tops, scraps, wild flowers and grasses were also pastimes, but cigarette cards were the favourite. They were free and plentiful. It was a great smoking era. You were not a man unless you smoked, and manhood could not come quickly enough when you were ten.

The cigarette manufacturers competed with each other and offered cards, coupons, competitions and free gifts, and made extravagant claims for their products to tempt the ardent smoker to another brand. The cards cumulated into sets of fifty. There were railway engines, flags of the nations, kings and queens, footballers and cricketers, famous actors and film stars. Duplicates were exchanged with your friends all eager to complete a set to stick into an album that cost an old penny from the tobacconist.

Wild Woodbines were the working man's "fags". Five

129

in a flimsy packet for twopence just fitted into the top pocket of a man's overall. Park Drive and Weights were contenders but Woodbines were supreme throughout the twenties and thirties, but for those higher up the social scale, Woodbines had a very definite working class label, and civil servants, skilled workers and clerical assistants usually smoked Players Navy Cut at eleven-pence (5p) for twenty. These were presented in a stouter packet carrying a portrait of a bearded sailor framed in a lifebuoy. Other popular brands were Wills' Gold Flake, Kensitas, or Craven "A", which appealed to the growing band of women smokers because the makers claimed that "they do not harm your throat".

My father always smoked Players Navy Cut and, if he commissioned one of us to fetch him a packet, we were allowed to keep the halfpenny change from a shilling. All attempts to persuade him to change to Black Cat, which gave away coupons that could be exchanged for a model train set, were of no avail. "You can't have good tobacco and free gifts," he contended, and it was no use "kicking up" — No meant No, but at Christmas a Hornby train set appeared for me and a Meccano construction set for my brother.

The following year a set of Lott's real stone bricks made it possible to build stations and signal boxes. Any birthday money was spent on extra track and other accessories. It was unfortunate with model railways then that everything had to be cleared away after each running session because it cluttered up the living room. Such expensive presents did not come often. For the most part we concocted our own toys. An unwanted shoebox, a pair of scissors and a tube of glue could produce a railway overbridge, a station, a toy theatre or a peep show, and we often saw girls from poor families dragging along a shoebox by a piece of string. It was a pram for a filthy rag doll. Wooden crates, broken beyond further use, could sometimes be scrounged from shop-keepers. We dismantled them and turned them into forts for lead soldiers, farmyards or fashioned them into boats.

Nothing was ever thrown away. "It might come in useful." Pieces of soap that had become too small for use in bathroom or sink were put into a soap saver; a wire mesh container with a long handle that hung near the kitchen sink. It was immersed in the washing up water and agitated to produce a lather. Brown paper from the week's groceries was smoothed, folded and stored against future requirements, knots in string were untied, the string rewound into hanks that were kept in the "string bag" behind the pantry door. The white paper used by the butcher could be smoothed out and used for drawing paper. To buy any of these items was regarded as reckless extravagance when they were supplied free.

There was a re-use for everything. Empty pop bottles were returned to the shopkeeper who gave a penny for each one. Astute youngsters were quick to take advantage of this by knocking on doors to ask if housewives had any empty bottles they wished to be rid of. It could be a lucrative trade. There were many ways for the shrewd to make a few coppers. They ran errands, chopped firewood and collected horse manure in buckets and sold them to those less inclined to do these things themselves.

Once the tradesmen's horse-drawn vehicles had completed their rounds the roads that were not bus routes were deserted and safe playgrounds for the street games that traffic has since made too dangerous. We were allowed out after tea until seven o'clock on the understanding that no games caused annoyance to neighbours and were not played near houses where anyone's father was "on nights" and likely to be in bed. Ball games were not encouraged because of the risks of breaking a window and the consequent stoppage of pocket money for many weeks to pay for the damage.

Each season came and went, defined not so much by the weather but by the games played. We played some games throughout the year; others were regulated by the availability of equipment. "Conkers" could only be played after the horse chestnuts had fallen and kites could only be flown during the windy weather of early spring. The conkers were baked hard in the oven and kites were concocted from thin pieces of wood, tissue paper and string. These preparations were all part of the fun.

Both sexes indulged in some of the games, others were the strict preserve of one or the other. No boy would have played Hop-scotch or any of the skipping games played by the girls. To have been seen doing so would have invited ridicule from one's friends. Girls did not play with conkers or a tip cat, which could be dangerous, neither did they play with marbles, but boys and girls spun tops or bowled hoops. Sometimes, if numbers were short, we invited the girls to join in a game of Release, which could be a rough game that involved being physically restrained from escaping from the "bases" at lamp posts and trees.

When we were very young we played round singing games; *In and out the windows*, *Nuts in May*, *What's the time, Mr Wolf* and *The Big Ship Sails on the Alley Alley O*. No-one knew what the Alley Alley O was, but it has been suggested that its origin lay in the opening of the Manchester Ship Canal. Most of the games involved someone being "It" and the elimination of the players one by one. There was a special thrill in these games during the dark winter months when we congregated in the pools of light shed by the flickering gas lamps.

The girls graduated to a variety of competitive games played with skipping ropes, or Hop-scotch played on a pitch of numbered squares chalked on the pavement into which the contestants kicked a flat piece of wood whilst hopping on one leg.

Curiosity over the mysteries of corking persuaded us to ask the girls to teach us how it was done but, before this could be accomplished we had to concoct a corking machine. It consisted of a disused cotton reel into one end of which were driven four nails. Strands of wool of various colours were then threaded in a complicated way round the nails and pushed down through the hole in the reel to emerge as a multi-coloured rope. Yards of this were made to be used in a variety of games. Reins for playing "horses" was one. Another was called Paddy, in which an empty cotton reel was threaded onto the rope which was tied into a circle and held by all players except "Paddy" who stood in the middle trying to spot the reel as it was passed surreptitiously along the rope from hand to hand while we sang. When "Paddy" succeeded in seeing the ring he changed places with whoever had held it.

During the marble season we carried our marbles in a small bag. It was held together at the top by a drawstring long enough for the bag to be carried over the shoulder. Anyone seen carrying a similar bag could be challenged to a game. It was dishonourable to refuse. There were two common marble games. In one a player rolled a marble along the gutter. His opponent tried to win it by rolling one of his marbles after it and hitting it. Complications and sometimes altercations resulted in the event of a marble being knocked into a drain. In the second game one player held a marble board; a piece of wood about twelve inches long in which openings sufficiently wide for a marble to pass through had been cut. Above each opening was a number. The board was held at an agreed distance by one player while the second attempted to roll marbles through the apertures. If he succeeded he won the number of marbles specified above the hole. Any marbles that did not pass through any holes were claimed by the opponent

Flicking, or skimming, cigarette cards was another popular game with the boys. There were several versions. You could win a card by flicking one of your own so that it landed on top of one previously flicked by an opponent, or you could stand a row of cards against a wall and let others try to win them by flicking their cards to knock them down. Tip-cat was another favourite, but it could be dangerous if the tip-cat hit anyone or flew against a window pane. The tip-cat was a stick about four inches long that had had its ends sharpened into points. It was laid on the ground and one of its ends struck with a longer stick which caused it to jump into the air. The skill lay in striking it a second time while it was in flight and sending it as far as possible.

Whips, tops, five stones and hoops were usually bought with pocket money because it was difficult to make sufficiently well-balanced ones at home. Sometimes an old motor tyre could be scrounged from a newly-opened garage in College Road. Such a hoop was envied by everyone. Diablos and yo-yos also had to be bought, usually by the more affluent as they cost sixpence each. Long jumps and jumping off walls with the aid of a clothes prop was another pastime if you could manage to sneak out of the house with one and without detection. On one occasion a broken prop had a disastrous effect on my brother's pocket money. Fortunately the prop broke into even lengths and, undismayed, he concocted a pair of stilts which provided an unexpected diversion.

The possessor of a mouth organ was in demand for musical games. A cheaper instrument was a Jew's harp; a piece of metal fashioned like a lyre with a projecting metal tongue which was held against partly-opened front teeth and twanged with the thumb to produce "music".

If, during a particularly hectic game, some respite were needed, a player became exhausted or felt exposed to unfair treatment, a truce could be declared by crossing the fingers and calling "Barley"; a truce word peculiar to the Birmingham area, and whenever it was used it was honoured without question and a game did not proceed until agreement had been reached.

In the evenings, play outside over, reading was our main diversion. At first it was the stories from *Chick's Own* read to us by our mother. These followed the adventures of a bright yellow chick and his friend, a black chick, who would have won approval from minority groups, but his name, "Nigger" would not. From here, once we could read, we graduated to *Rainbow* and the Rupert Bear stories in hardback at one shilling (5p) which became part of our childhood mythology and were welcome birthday presents.

Once we were able to read, every available piece of printed material that came into the house was eagerly devoured. The daily newspapers all carried a strip cartoon for children and we followed the adventures of the Arkubs in the *News Chronicle*, and Pip, Squeak and Wilfred in the *Daily Mirror*. As we grew older tastes veered towards what our mother termed "ridiculous" reading. These were the penny comics; *Funny Wonder*, *Jester* and *Comic Cuts*, but in her tolerance we were allowed to buy one each week which, once digested, was "swopped" at school for a different one.

Later we gravitated to the twopenny weeklies and again by "swopping" we read all five of the most popular weeklies; *Hotspur*, *Rover*, *Skipper*, *Wizard* and *Adventure*, which were more acceptable at home because they featured sport, romantic history, tales of lost cities and futuristic voyages.

The more incredible the stories the more they were

enjoyed; death rays, improbable machines, giant robots, interplanetary cruises by methods of propulsion left vague. Britain, if not in danger from foreign hordes or Martians, was always the one hope of the world.

There was one comic that we were forbidden to bring into the house. This was *The Bullseye* which had to be smuggled in and read surreptitiously under the bed-clothes. It was the last of the "penny dreadfuls" and the most thrilling reading. Lurid tales rich with anach-ronisms and bristling with horror abounded. Frightening men with glaring eyes, hooded terrors and masked unknowns lurked in dark alleys and fog-shrouded graveyards. Gaping tombs, haunted granges and mys-terious casks were plentiful, and phantoms and vampire bats infested charnel houses and fatal closets. It was compulsive reading that did us no harm. These travesties of Gothic tales were so improbable that they implanted no ideas to imitate.

What we read, nevertheless, coloured our views and affected our thinking. We didn't know what a public school was but devoured the stories in *The Magnet* and *Gem* without feeling jealous or envious. They were just stories we relished. These and the stories in other magazines set standards and we developed a sense of right and wrong. We felt no outrage if characters were birched or flogged for stealing someone's tuck box. Stealing was stealing and thieves were thieves. They were not victims of society, social misfits, or deprived.

Rightly or wrongly crime and punishment were not matters we debated. Foreigners, however, were in a different category. Anyone (according to the magazines,

137

books and eventually films available to us) who was not British and white was one of these foreigners. They lived a long way off and were peculiar, grotesque even in some cases. The dark-skinned races were, for the most part, lovable coons, their image promoted by the comics and enhanced by the seaside chocolate-coloured coons and nigger minstrel shows. "Sambo" and "Golliwog" were terms of endearment not insults.

Melodramatic fiction conjured up visions of the evil designs of an opium-ridden Chinese nation hell-bent on torturing and "Shanghai-in" Englishmen. Egyptians and Indians, with few exceptions, were sinister, ungrateful people, "fiendishly cunning" and forever wanting to wage war on those who had brought them the multifold blessings of civilisation. As foreigners and immigrants were far too few for any of us ever to meet and foreign travel was unattainable to us, these impressions endured. The British way of life was an example for the peoples of the world to follow. If they didn't want it then it was our sacred duty to show them that way and, if necessary, to enforce it.

Despite the fact that wireless aerials had begun to appear in neighbouring gardens it was not until the early 1930s that my father, ever cautious and suspicious of all things new, could be persuaded to invest in a wireless set. Until the late 1920s the only ones we had heard had been on visits to relatives to listen to the novelties concocted by uncles who were sufficiently dedicated to produce a "cat's whisker" crystal set with earphones. These were not very satisfactory. There were only two sets of earphones and these were passed around so no-one ever heard a complete programme, but that was not of great importance. It was the novelty of listening to voices from afar that appealed. A loudspeaker on the mantle-piece was a later improvement, but the constant inter-ruptions, ear-splitting crackles and blurring by atmospheric interference soon detracted from the initial enjoyment.

In my father's opinion wireless was insufficiently advanced, and it was not until the arrival of the "super-het" all mains sets that were complete in themselves, encased in a polished plywood box with a fretwork front and advertised as "table models" that he was convinced. After consultations with friends and relatives who had recently acquired a set a decision was made to buy a Marconi. "After all," my Father pronounced naively, "he invented wireless so they must be the best."

Not everyone could take advantage of the new all mains sets because most of the older houses in the city had not been wired for electricity, but this could be over-come by hiring a battery that had to be carried to the nearest garage or electrical shop periodically to be recharged. These latest inventions cost around twenty pounds; the equivalent of several weeks wages, but, somehow, most households managed to acquire one chosen from a range of British-made Echo, Ultra or Marconi sets that were appearing in the specialist shops such as Matty's that had begun to open in suburban High Streets.

Some people who could not afford, or did not care, to make an outright payment took advantage of a hire purchase scheme; an innovation calculated to stimulate spending and create work. The system was disparaged by the majority, who had been taught that what they could not afford had to be saved for or done without. The stigma of buying something on the "never never" took a long time to die.

Once the wireless set had been installed, photography, woodwork and my father's other erstwhile pastimes, were curtailed to accommodate the new pastime of "listening in", and domestic habits were changed so that we could all settle down to enjoy cosy fireside evenings as new worlds in the imagination were opened up.

The cinema was the silver screen of the 1930s but the wireless was its golden voice. Listening in was an adventure. Never before had we been able to be entertained professionally and spontaneously in our own home, and influenced from beyond its immediate surroundings by the well-informed and unbiased. Stephen King-Hall spoke on current affairs, Malcolm Sargent and Walford Davies encouraged us to appreciate music and Mr Middleton (his Christian name was not revealed) advised on gardening. His Sunday mid-day talks invariably included references to manure spreading as we were consuming the Sunday lunch. My mother was of the opinion that the BBC ought to ask him to be a little more considerate at a time when the nation was sitting down to enjoy the principal meal of the week.

Despite the advances that had been made there was still some interference in reception, and the elimination of atmospherics, oscillations and superheterodyne whistles necessitated a certain amount of knob twiddling. The *Radio Times* (price twopence) with its detailed programmes, articles and renowned illustrations, was indispensable for full enjoyment. We were able to receive two programmes, the National and the Midland, which was broadcast from the BBC's studios in Broad Street.

The day's programme always began with the morning service, but there was rarely any daytime listening in our home because it not only encouraged idleness but also cost electricity. Listening began when we rushed in from school to enjoy Children's Hour, especially the sheer delight of *Toytown* with the magical voices of Mr Growser, the Mayor and Derek McCulloch as Larry the lamb that have never been matched on television. Neither has Romany who, with his dog Rags, brought the countryside to life so vividly in his imaginary walks. You forgot "the set" in the world of broadcast fantasy conjured up in the serials and in the mental pictures created by the sound effects of marching hordes, dripping caves, echoing dungeons, clanging gates and howling gales.

The early evening news was essential listening. After that, especially when homework was of paramount importance, the wireless was switched off, but anticipation of the evening's programme was the incentive to dispose of the homework as quickly as possible so that we could enjoy the adaptations of famous plays and original ones, many by L. Du Garde Peach and Mabel Constanduros, who created the lovable Cockney Buggins Family; and there were musicals, *Wild Violets*,

141

The Student Prince, *Cavalcade* and many specially-written ones.

Saturday evening was the highlight of the week when we settled down with a sixpenny tin of Meeson's toffees as the voice of a Piccadilly flowerseller and the noise of London's traffic was abruptly halted to bring us some of the interesting people who were *In Town Tonight*. A galaxy of talent followed in *Music Hall* that sought to entertain without offence to anyone. Lord Reith was guided by his own rules of unbiased and inoffensive broadcasting. I was not very interested in the slapstick comedy and preferred the sophistication of the Western Brothers and Gillie Potter's continuing saga of the village of Hoggs Norton, but I enjoyed the gossipy reflections of Gert and Daisy and the Midland programme of *Aerbut and Gaertie*, who poked gentle fun at neighbours, local customs and events in the Birmingham dialect.

By contrast the Sunday programmes, until evening, were restricted to religious services, serious music or uplifting talks. Only on Radio Luxembourg was there a leavening of popular recordings but, in households with any pretence at respectability, this was frowned upon. Such music was not, in my mother's opinion, suitable for Sundays, but *The Table under the Tree*, which followed the evening service, was an enjoyable programme of light classical music played "somewhere in Italy" with a commentary by the "Man in the Cloak", but the big attraction for us was the twelve-instalment serial play; *The Count of Monte Cristo*, *Les Miserables*, *Vanity Fair* and many other celebrated novels that were brought to life for us and laid the foundations for a lasting love of literature.

Not so popular at home were the big dance bands, but some of our teenage friends were sometimes able to persuade their parents to let them roll up the carpet so that we could dance to the music of Ambrose, Jack Payne or Henry Hall. Dancing was not encouraged by my father. It was "the kind of thing that savages do." Even my mother, who had enjoyed waltzing and the Lancers in her Edwardian youth, deplored the decline of the violin, declaring with some asperity that in her day a saxophone would have stood as little chance of getting into a dance orchestra as a mouth organ.

Such was the influence of the wireless that people feared for the future of theatres, cinemas, libraries and even the dance halls. The reverse was the case. The listeners flocked to see the plays and films they had heard and wanted to read the books. Dance band fans besieged the local dance halls when popular bands were appearing. Programmes like *Scrapbook* and *Talks in the Train* stimulated discussion and, although it was barely perceptible, the wireless began slowly, very slowly, to erode the barriers that existed between the classes of society as people became more educated and articulate.

The view from the back bedroom windows was un-inspiring; garden fences, grey roofs, chimney pots and wireless aerials; until one morning the skyline was dramatically changed.

An apex of steel girders appeared beyond the roof tops. A detour to school had to be made to satisfy curiosity. A cinema was in course of construction; its lower half at an advanced stage. With the nearest cinemas at Erdington and Perry Barr, and at distances sufficient to discourage all but the most determined on winter evenings, a captive audience was assured.

The *Mayfair* was not as awe-inspiring as some of the suburban cinemas that were being built as the age of the super cinema dawned. In architecture it could not compete with the Moorish palaces, Greek temples and Gothic cathedrals, grandly named the *Regal*, *Imperial*, *Empress*, *Palace* or *Plaza*, some designed to lure audiences with promises of organ recitals on a magnificent electric Wurlitzer that rose, spotlighted, from beneath the proscenium arch during the ice cream interval for the resident organist to delight with selections from popular musical plays, interspersed with his own compositions to demonstrate both his versatility and the effects that could be created with the organ.

The super cinemas with their lavish decor of marble staircases, tinkling fountains, glittering chandeliers and resplendent uniformed staffs extended the dream world of the screen and provided exotic settings in which we watched the Hollywood adventures. They lent an atmosphere of luxury far removed from the real world that surrounded us.

The *Mayfair* had no organ but was impressive enough with its blue and gold box office foyer and twin flight of stairs that led to an upper foyer and thence to the balcony seats at one and sixpence (7p). Programmes were changed on Mondays and Thursdays, with a matinee on Wednesdays and a "tuppenny rush" for children on

Saturday afternoons, when the house was filled with noisy youngsters who seemed to be in perpetual transit taking even younger ones to the toilets and missing out on some of the antics of Harold Lloyd, Charlie Chaplin or Laurel and Hardy. A Micky Mouse cartoon was an essential ingredient of the programme, followed by a cowboy film featuring Tom Mix or one about Rin Tin Tin, a dog who saved his master from a thousand deaths. A cliff-hanging serial, leaving the juvenile audience in suspense over a hero or heroine in a burning building, dangling over a roaring torrent or about to be scalped by Red Indians, ended the performance and ensured next week's audience.

Saturday night was the highlight of the week for many and in the early evening we watched from the living room window to see who was "going to the pictures". Even during the depression most of the estate's population managed one weekly visit to the *Mayfair* where, in the warmth and the luxury of seats more comfortable than many had in their homes, they escaped from the realities of the world outside to the glamour of the Hollywood spectacles, tear-jerking romances or the gyrations of Fred Astaire and Ginger Rogers.

All was fantasy. There were few British films and only one, featuring Gracie Fields, drew attention to the working class. The others, which included a few memorable historical dramas, depicted a monied and leisured class where any lower orders were portrayed as comical Cockneys or slow-witted Northerners. No-one lived in a council house or rode on a tram. The film makers had got it right. People did not want to be reminded of their circumstances while they were escaping from them in a world of make-believe where no film could offend. There was a strict Board of Censorship, a Lord Chamberlain to be satisfied and, in Birmingham, an even stricter Watch Committee, ensured that there was no titillation beyond the bounds of decency.

We were not regular cinema goers, but on occasion the fireside, the wireless and the sixpenny tin of Meeson's toffees were abandoned for a Saturday evening's entertainment at the *Mayfair*. On the steps a commissionaire, resplendent in a uniform of blue decorated with gold braid, exercised his authority. One of his duties was to patrol the queue and chastise children who were not allowed in unless accompanied by an adult but who tried to infiltrate the queue alongside sympathetic-looking adults with a plea of "Will you take us in Mister?" Excitedly we waited for the curtains to part. Before the main film came a short feature and the Pathe Gazette, a newsreel showing the world's events of the previous week. In a pre-television era this was avidly digested. The selected films we were taken to see introduced us to some of the dramas of history and the classics.

David Copperfield, A Tale of Two Cities and *Cardinal Richelieu* were unforgettable for the scenes and characters. The films were nearly all American-made but leavened by a fair sprinkling of actors and actresses; Madeleine Carroll, Greta Garbo, Marlene Dietrich and others imported from England, Scandinavia and Germany. By today's standards those films might be judged as inexpert but were acclaimed as triumphs at the time, and all of us who saw the first version of *Vanity Fair* can recall the skilful use of colour in this first all-talkie technicolour production.

Over the next few years we saw *The Scarlet Pimpernel*, *Wuthering Heights*, *Anna Karenina* and H.G. Wells' *Things to Come*, an alarmingly prophetic film with startling effects by an inventive genius. There were many films that glorified the Empire; *Rhodes of Africa*, *The Lives of a Bengal Lancer* and *Clive of India* that would be derided nowadays as blatant imperialism but then they were rapturously received. It was half a century before *Gandhi* revealed a different aspect of British life in the Empire; an aspect that few would have credited fifty years ago.

Recovery and Prosperity 1934

"I shan't be in this afternoon," declared Mrs Murgatroyd as she handed the customary cup of tea over the garden fence one day.

This was a startling revelation by one who rarely strayed beyond the estate's confines, except on a Saturday evening when, in the company of Mr Murgatroyd, she made an excursion to sample the delights of the recently-opened *Golden Cross* at Short Heath. "I'm going to see my sister, Alice, an' I'll tell you for why," she confided with the air of one announcing an event of grave national importance. "They say 'er creates (makes a fuss) because I never go," she continued, evidently feeling obliged to explain her impulsive intention. "'Er only lives a tuppenny tram!"

Mrs Murgatroyd's estimation of distances was not specified by mileage, but by the time taken on foot or the amount expended in fares to accomplish a journey. By a strange quirk of Fate on that particular afternoon, Mrs Murgatroyd's sister decided to take time by the forelock to travel in the opposite direction to surprise Mrs Murgatroyd. Receiving no reply to her knocking and, peering through the window, detecting no sign of life, she called at our house to try to discover a reason for her sister's eccentricity. "She never goes out of an afternoon," she affirmed and, refreshed by a freshly-brewed cup of tea, she settled down in our living room to await her sister's return.

It was some two hours later that Mrs Murgatroyd returned from her abortive mission. If her sister, Alice, had anticipated a tender reunion she was about to be disappointed. Mrs Murgatroyd's astonishment at seeing her sister emerge from our house was only exceeded by her greeting. "Why, our Alice, don't you never do no such thing again," she chided. "Between us we've wasted eight pence in tram fares. Enough to buy two loaves."

There was no saving grace in Mrs Murgatroyd's treatment of her relations, but her attitude was typical of many who had to manage on a less than average income. Money was a commodity in scarce supply and there was no spare bread to cast upon the waters. Anything in the nature of a treat had to be balanced carefully against the essential requirements of a family and the fares involved in travelling to and from work from an estate remote from the factories that had been previously reached by walking, even though the corporation, bearing this in mind, had deliberately kept fares low from outlying areas.

The plight of Mrs Murgatroyd struggling to nourish a family of seven on a low income was that of many Birmingham families juggling with between three and four pounds a week, which was considered to be a living wage. Nobody's cup was overflowing, but it was possible with careful budgeting to enjoy a reasonable standard of living. In our home the drive and initiative was supplied by a bright and bustling mother, who was a good housewife, cook and needlewoman. She made all our clothes and most of her own until, with the insensitivity of youth we demanded ready to wear garments like everyone else. It was ever thus; to be like the herd. It did not occur to us that it was through our mother's resourcefulness that we were able to enjoy the treats that were denied to others. Good food, within the constraints of the housekeeping allowance, was a prerequisite; it was the monotony and lack of variety that sometimes jaded our appetites, but we always had a good pudding and food, we were frequently reminded, was for nourishment and not gourmandising. You ate what was offered or went without. There were no convenience foods that could be instantly produced, and the idea of cooking an alternative was not, even for the most fastidious, considered. It would have been far too wasteful with gas supplied from a penny-in the-slot meter.

The economies practised by capable housewives were simple commonsense. Clothes were never cast aside because they had become old-fashioned but only when they were beyond repair. Sheets that had worn thin in the middle were subjected to a "sides to middle" sewing operation to prolong their lives. These operations all helped to keep a family respectable in the eyes of others. "Respectable" was one of the three other "R's" that were drummed into us. We had to be "respectable" in dress and grooming, to "respect" property and be "respectful" to other people, but never to consider we were better than others; more fortunate maybe but certainly not better.

*　　*　　*

The early years of the 1930s saw the little estate at its zenith and some of the amenities that people had clamoured for became realities. Our mothers had no cars to transport commodities in bulk from supermarket to freezer, but no longer needed to hump groceries and vegetables from the shops unless they could not afford the extra penny charged for delivery.

By now the estate was well-served by roundsmen. Groceries were delivered by the grocery boy on a bicycle from orders placed earlier in the week. The milkman began to deliver milk in bottles instead of dispensing it from a churn on his float. The baker called each day and greengrocer and coalman weekly. Uniformed gas and electricity officials rode around on their bicycles to collect the money from the meters. Most of the delivery vehicles were horse-drawn and children were cautioned to "Mind the 'orses." The refuse collection vehicles were an innovation and Birmingham was a pioneer in using electrically-propelled dust carts.

On hot-summer days a man on a tricycle with a box between the two front wheels pedalled his way round the estate ringing a bell and crying "Eldorado." He was not heralding the arrival of the promised golden age but merely proclaiming the superiority of his ice cream over that of his rival "Midland Counties".

With the constant procession of tradesmen and the window cleaners, chimney sweeps, insurance men and other door to door salesmen, there was little opportunity for thieves. There were too many people around for detection to be unnoticed. Maybe it was because few had anything worth stealing or there were no fast getaway cars but it was more likely to have been the rigid standards set by our parents that discouraged any criminal behaviour, and few things disturbed the peace of the estate.

There were minor sensations; sudden deaths, births and unexpected removals to hospital, but only one that outraged society. A bus driver's wife who ran off with another man leaving a distraught husband and children. It was unprecedented. The news ran round the estate like quick-silver causing Mrs Lamoney to remark with affected indifference "It's just what you might expect from them in Capilano Road," and thereby castigating unjustifiably a whole section of the community. "It's beyond my comprehension," she concluded. It was beyond most people's. One married for better or for worse, and if it turned out to be for worse it had to be borne with fortitude, but for a mother to leave her children and a husband who worked shifts was almost beyond belief. The only single parent families were those of widows who could expect some relief from the State. For a man whose wife had left him there was nothing.

But all was not gloom and uncertainty; a wasteland of frustrated hopes. As the decade progressed there was an improvement in the country's economy and many more jobs materialised in the ever-growing motor and construction industries. Perry Common had at last acquired some kind of identity. When asked where you lived, people no longer asked "What Common?", "Where's that?" or made ribald comments about "very common".

We now had a church hall, albeit a wooden structure, that could be used for meetings, concerts and dances.

The *Mayfair* cinema had been built equipped for the "talkies" at a time when many other cinemas had been closed temporarily to be wired for sound and their orchestras and pianists replaced by mighty Wurlitzers that rose bathed in shimmering light from the depths. The *Crossways* public house, at the corner of College and Hawthorn Roads, opened its doors. The long-awaited public library was erected on the site of the old school cherry orchard opposite the Jacobean-style public house and, to avoid any possible confusion between them, was built in a restrained Georgian-style of architecture. Both obviated long walks and became popular resorts and meeting places for those who thirsted but for different reasons.

On the fringes of the estate there was plenty of entertainment, much of it free. Most local firms held sports and gala days for the families and friends of employees. The GEC, Kynoch's (now IMI) and the Tramways Department had operatic and dramatic societies which gave performances in their respective canteens where you could enjoy, for the price of a programme, an evening of three one-act plays or a Gilbert and Sullivan opera, and there were concerts in the parks where Police and Fire Brigade bands gave frequent performances.

The Band of the Salvation Army sometimes performed in the School Hall and when it was rumoured that the Band of Hope was coming I, together with a group of friends, sought permission from wry-smiling parents, to attend. We had not heard of this "Hope Band"

153

but made our way to the School Hall in anticipation of trumpet voluntaries and cornet solos. A little dark spare man with a dolorous expression ushered us in. The hall filled up, mainly with expectant juveniles. There was no sign of a band but a female equipped with a pair of pince-nez spectacles and an indomitable expression took a seat on the rostrum. She was joined by the little dark spare man who prayed silence for Mrs Sedge.

Mrs Sedge rose majestically, throwing open her coat to reveal an operatic chest encased in a blue dress, the uppermost part decorated with an expanse of brown embroidery. "She looks like an old piano with a fretwork front," muttered a man in the row behind us and, as we tried to stifle our amusement, she began "Tonight we are going to talk about the hygiene of food and drink." A look of bewilderment spread across our faces. This was not what we had expected, but there was not now any escape. The doors were firmly closed and guarded by a sentinel with a "Don't you dare" expression on his countenance. So we listened to a lecture that had little to do with food but much concerning drink.

Our innocence was shattered as we learnt that things are not always what they seem. We grasped that drink was the servant of Satan and a disciple of the Devil. If we rejected strong drink Mrs Sedge promised us Nirvana, if not, the flames of hell. We didn't know what Nirvana was but it sounded preferable to the fires of hell. At the end of Mrs Sedge's homily, the little dark spare man, whose sole contribution so far had been to sit at her side nodding like a mandarin at some of her dire predictions, gave pencils and paper to all children present and we were commanded to report the lecture.

After an appropriate interval our efforts were collected and we were invited to sign what Mrs Sedge referred to as "The Pledge" but, not fully understanding its nature and having been forewarned by our parents, who were wiser than we were, not to sign anything, most of us declined. A few weeks later and through the post came a certificate to the effect that I had satisfied the examiners in reporting a lecture on the hygiene of food and drink. Such success did not encourage me to attend any future meetings of the Band.

Things continued to improve throughout the 1930s despite a deteriorating situation in Europe; a chancellor murdered in Austria and clashes between various political factions in far away countries. They seemed of little significance to us at the time. Mr Baldwin was back as Prime Minister and Mr Churchill was clamouring for rearmament which was to provide more jobs, but not, it seemed, for the Murgatroyds. Their Minnie got married and with her went her contribution to the family's finances.

"Our Raymon' can't get a job," Mrs Murgatroyd asserted one day with the uninflected accents of doom. "Says 'e's going to join the Army." It was the choice of many school leavers who were unable to find jobs but were lured by such popular songs as *There's something about a soldier*. The Army promised them a great life with all the ingredients of excitement denied them in civilian life. Vast armies were maintained at prodigious expense all over India, parts of Africa, the Far East and

Palestine to maintain order and contain threatened eruptions. It was all very necessary to maintain British superiority which none doubted. So our Raymon' went off to Woolwich.

It was through our parents good management, that sometimes amounted to frugality, that we were able to enjoy much that others were denied. There were the exhibitions. We never missed the Brighter Homes Exhibition at Bingley Hall, where the entrance fee was soon recouped by the exhibitors free samples of food and drink, badges and booklets. There were miniature *Hovis* loaves to take home, slugs of linotype set with your name while you waited and presented by the linotype operators on the *Birmingham Mail* stand. Thoughtful exhibitors provided you with a carrier bag to transport the loot. All this for sixpence (less than 3p) and against a colourful display by the "Dancing Fountains" to the accompaniment of the *Skaters Waltz* or the *Poet and Peasant Overture*.

Later in the year, also for sixpence, you could visit the British Industries Fair at Castle Bromwich; a showcase for the city's products represented by working models, machines and free books and brochures.

In the summer of 1928 we went to London to stay with friends and visit some of my mother's relations and then on to the seaside for a further week. It was the farthest we had ever been. Our father did not come with us. It would have been impracticable for him to have taken the time off and forfeit two weeks' wages, but Kynoch's must have been early pioneers in awarding holidays with

156

pay because, in subsequent years, we all went away for one week's holiday every year.

There was frenzied activity during the weeks preceding the London adventure. New clothes for my brother and me and new dresses for our mother had to be made on her treadle-operated sewing machine. She was always smartly dressed and never far behind with fashion, although she deplored the fact that skirt hems had risen so high that they almost showed a woman's knees.

She returned from town one day, whence she had been with Mrs Sandell, a friend she had made through the Women's Guild, to see their first talking film, Al Jolson in *The Singing Fool*, wearing what she called a cloche hat. It had a brim so low on her forehead that she found it difficult to see ahead. It was, of course, the very latest fashion, but worse was disclosed when she removed it to reveal her "bobbed" hair. She had been shorn of her tresses that had hitherto hung down to her waist when uncoiled. All discarded to satisfy the fashion of short hair that could be shingled, semi-shingled, Eton-cropped or crimped into "Marcel" waves. She had treated my brother and me to "Christopher Robin" felt hats (as worn by that character in A.A. Milne's stories). We hated them. Why couldn't we wear caps like other boys? but in London, it seemed, things were different and nothing must give the impression that provincials were dowdy and unfashionable.

Excitement mounted as we travelled on the Great Western Express from Snow Hill to Paddington to begin a glorious week of entertainment and exploration. We rode on an escalator, a tube train and an electric one out to Croydon, where we saw an Imperial Airways flight land from Paris. We were only allowed to stay for a few minutes after it had landed because of the danger from the noxious exhaust fumes. The Horseguards we saw in Whitehall were so still that we asked "Are they real?" From there we went to see the guards marching in front of the railings at Buckingham Palace in the days before the tourists had driven them inside the Palace Yard but, of all the sights we saw, none thrilled us more than the zoo.

We went on to the Kent coast, but our first view of the sea was disappointing. The weather was not good, the sea was grey not blue and the golden sand we expected to see was all pebbles and not at all like the pictures we had seen in books, but the initial disappointment with the seaside was overcome in subsequent years when we went to Bridlington or Weston-Super-Mare.

Two and a half guineas (£2.62p) was the typical rate for one for a week's holiday at a private hotel with full board, and the twenty five pounds budgeted for the family holiday included treats of toys, ice creams and a ride to Cheddar or Scarborough on one of the charabancs that lined the promenade kerbside. At Weston-Super-Mare a simple pleasure was a ride along the sea front on the open top deck of an antiquated tramcar; an oddity that had disappeared from the streets at home. One year some excitement was provided by a man carrying a copy of the *News Chronicle* who strutted along the promenade masquerading as "Lobby Lud" expecting to be accosted by someone else who also carried a copy of that day's

News Chronicle. If the correct challenge "You are Lobby Lud. I claim the *News Chronicle* prize" were given "Lobby Lud" would hand over a one-pound note. The objective, to increase the sales of the newspaper, supplied entertainment for the hopeful stalkers and embarrassment to the innocent promenaders who happened to be clutching a copy of the newspaper.

In the winter theatre-going was a special treat. There were eight professional theatres in town. We usually went to the *Theatre Royal, the Prince of Wales* or the *Alexandra*, which had recently been re-built, and saw the Aldwych farces, *The Desert Song, Bitter Sweet, Chu Chin Chow* and other popular musicals or revivals of the era. Smoking during the performance was encouraged by the provision of an ashtray screwed to the back of cach seat and ladies were "kindly requested to remove their hats" which might, otherwise, obscure the view of those in the row behind.

For these occasions it was very necessary to dress properly. Before the time that jeans and trainers became almost univcrsal dress for any occasion, dressing appropriately under different circumstances was an obligation. It was an essential element in life in whatever class you found yourself.

Wardrobes were very basic and clothes, especially those for men, were generally dull. Everyone wore a hat. For men it was probably not so much as a decoration but to protect their hair, greased with "Brilliantine", from the filth that fell from the skies, but no man would have worn jewellery other than a watch chain or a discreet signet ring. There were a few departures from standard dress; some of our older fashion-conscious cousins invested in plus-fours, and one eccentric uncle sported a pair of spats, but our amusement prevented us from enquiring whether these were intended to keep his ankles warm or his shoes from becoming spattered with mud. It was not until hiking became a popular pastime that there was any relaxation. For hiking a special dress was essential; khaki shorts and an open-necked shirt were as necessary as the haversack and the beret or a red handkerchief worn pirate-like. A new freedom in dress was dawning. Hitherto if a man did not wear a tie it was because he was too poor to own one.

We boys wore short trousers until we reached the magical age of fourteen. There were plenty of scratched and cut knees covered with bandages that were constantly slipping down onto our socks. At fourteen we suddenly became men, irrespective of physique, and those who left school to go to work were treated to a suit from the Fifty Shilling Tailors, who offered a three-piece suit for the equivalent of two pounds fifty. Those of us who stayed on at one of the grammar schools were put into long grey flannels and a school blazer. Anyone appearing at school without a tie, even on the warmest of days, was despatched home to find one. There was no way of circumventing the obligations to a class and dress conscious society without incurring censure.

Despite such irritating restrictions which we generally accepted, although not always without complaint, the early thirties were happy and memorable years. But events that were about to change the character and identity of Perry Common lay just over the horizon.

To the North and East farmland was being swallowed up in the development of vast new municipal estates. Warren Farm, Pheasey Farm, Welshman's Hill and the fields that stretched towards Oscott College disappeared and were covered with new houses being erected under an improvement and slum clearance scheme. The new houses showed many advances over those built twelve years earlier. They had tiled "Triplex" fireplaces in their living rooms and were equipped with hot water systems. They had "New World" gas cookers, and many had front parlours.

The thirty thousandth council house was opened by the Minister for Housing and we all went to see one of the new houses equipped by the corporation as an "all electric house" to extol the virtues of electricity for convenience and the reduction of pollution. We expected to see electric lights and fires, but were fascinated by the electric clocks, vacuum cleaners, toasters, blankets, washing machines and various "plug-in" devices destined to become commonplace in the future. "It looks like Paradise to me," remarked a woman. "Soon there'll be no work for us to do."

Before the decade was through, Perry Common was almost encircled. Only the cemetery wall and the Bleak Hills had prevented expansion to the South, and the centre of gravity was shifting northwards to where more shops, public houses, churches, community halls, swimming baths and a new cinema were being built. The various estates, at first named after the farms on whose land they had been built, were eventually welded together and named Kingstanding; taking its name from a small clump of trees where Charles I, on his way to the Battle of Edgehill in 1642 had held "a kind of Court at the King's Standing on Perry Common". Encirclement of the original estate was completed by private developments on the Bleak Hills and Warren Hill. Perry Common had ceased to be an island.

A Basic Education

"Not a mile from this school stands a farm where a man was caught forging money," began Mr Hinchley, the Headmaster of the newly-opened school in Hawthorn Road. "The farm is still there. The man's name was Booth and the 'Brummagem buttons', as his counterfeited coins were called, gave the town a bad name." He paused and glanced round the class through the gold-rimmed spectacles supported on his florid features to make sure that he had everyone's attention before unfolding his tale of the notorious Birmingham coiner.

His soft speaking voice and enthusiasm had a compelling quality and, by concentrating on familiar places and their associations with Baskerville, Hutton, Priestley, Boulton and a host of other characters he brought the city's history to life in his weekly talks to our class. The bombardment of Aston Hall, Sir Thomas Holte and his involvement with the Civil War served as an introduction to the nation's history, which was a mixture of undoubted facts and doubtful legends concerning kings who burned cakes, lost their jewels or commanded the tides to retreat.

The school in Hawthorn Road (as the lane was now called) was an extension to the one in Hastings Road which had become so overcrowded that by 1928 the junior girls had to be accommodated in some barrack-like huts that had been erected on nearby wasteland and a Miss Gammon was appointed as Headmistress, but the boys were even less fortunate. We were segregated from the girls for the rest of our school lives and moved away into forbidding-looking buildings that had once been a fever isolation hospital.

We entered the school grounds through a narrow gate in a high wall that screened the corrugated iron buildings that had been the hospital wards. Few alterations had been carried out and the erstwhile wards were divided into classrooms by curtains, which made concentration difficult, especially if the lesson being conducted behind the curtain proved to be more interesting than the one to which we were supposed to be attentive. A large cast iron coke-burning stove stood in the middle of each room. Those seated near to it suffered from excessive heat while those furthest away shivered from the lack of it. The stoves were difficult to regulate, gave off noxious fumes and had to be stoked and raked out several times a day, but these conditions had to be accepted. We all knew that we did not attend school to indulge in luxury but to become equipped with sufficient knowledge to earn a living. Truancy was rare and, apart from illnesses, absences were few. There were no amusement arcades with batteries of fruit machines to provide distractions and cover from detection, and a fear of the consequences of returning home soon led to boredom and a return to school. Visits to the homes of absentees by the "School Board man", as the Schools Inspector was still called, ensured that truancy was not a profitable pastime.

All our teachers were dedicated and responsible people who had received a better education than most of the parents of their pupils. They were always well-dressed and groomed. Their authority was absolute and unquestioned by pupils and parents. Answering back, impertinence or dumb insolence were neither expected nor tolerated and, although corporal punishment was permitted, I do not recall any incident where it was administered. The teaching staff had the support of parents, some of whom had not had any formal education beyond the age of ten but were not without the intellect to appreciate its benefits. Violence against teachers was not imagined. Such an eventuality would have outraged teachers, pupils and parents.

Mindful of the uncongenial conditions of the classrooms, advantage was taken during warm weather to hold classes in the extensive grounds surrounding the school. These stretched along College Road and Hawthorn Road behind the high brick wall. In the corner where the public library was subsequently built a cherry orchard flourished. We were forbidden to climb the trees or pick the fruit, and cherry pickers arrived each season to gather the crop for the city's hospitals. Elsewhere woodland paths led through glades where the lessons were held. The grounds had not been maintained for many years. The edges of the paths had crumbled and the flower beds were overgrown, but it was an exciting wonderland to explore and learn the names of the trees and wild flowers that flourished there.

School was popular, not only in anticipation of learning new facts, but also because there were few distractions outside. It was also a source of entertainment where sports, singing and acting were encouraged. Few homes had a wireless (as the radio was called).

Theatres and cinemas were too far away and, in most cases, too expensive for many people. There was, however, one daily entertainment provided by that novelty, the internal-combustion engine. This was in a car owned by Mrs Maude, the only teacher to possess one. There were no married women teachers then. A woman automatically resigned on marriage to look after a home and bring up a family, but Mrs Maude was a widow who wore her hair in two plaits which she coiled over her ears like a pair of earphones. Her fame rested not so much on her teaching ability but on the possession of a car; a rarity then. Her early black and yellow Austin stood outside the school, an object of ridicule. Such scoffing was in reality ill-concealed envy as each evening after the close of school a small group lingered to await the owner's emergence to watch with fascination the hand cranking of the engine and the manipulation of the knobs and levers that jolted it into life. It jerked, backfired and lurched off down Perry Common Road leaving behind a cloud of exhaust gas into which a group of "sniffers" plunged to indulge in the simple pleasure of inhaling the acrid fumes of hydrocarbons and carbon monoxide. It was an exhilarating experience, but air pollution was not then an issue of major concern. There were far more pressing problems to worry over than what came out of a car's exhaust pipe.

Morning began with a religious assembly in two classrooms temporarily converted to an assembly hall by drawing back the curtain partition. It was a ritual attended by everyone. There were no ethnic minorities whose sensitivities had to be considered. The hymns we sang were those of simple faith and love; *The King of Love my Shepherd is*, *Loving Shepherd of thy Sheep*, but we couldn't understand why there was "a green hill far away without a city wall". Why did a green hill need a city wall? We didn't ask and no-one explained that "without" could also mean "outside". It was much easier to understand that there was :

> The rich man in his castle,
> The poor man at his gate,
> He made them high or lowly
> And ordered their estate

. . . although it is doubtful if such simple faith would be accepted nowadays, but it was a time when self-sacrifice, service and a sense of duty were the dominant strands in our elementary education. Putting others before self was instilled into us and exemplified by Sir Henry Newbolt's exhortations to "Play up, play up and play the game," Rupert Brooke's reminder of heroic corners in foreign lands that were "forever England", Kipling's jingoism and the singing of *Land of Hope and Glory* at a time when there seemed little hope and even less glory for the majority.

We were taught that responsibilities rather than rights were paramount, and the importance of hard work, thrift and good manners was drilled into us, but excitement overcame good manners on an unforgettable morning in

May 1930 when a boy whose attention had wandered to the window cried out ecstatically "Oh, Sir, look!"

Mr Hewlett followed his gaze and, instead of an expected admonishment rapped "Everyone outside quickly." We scampered from our desks to find every-one else had done the same to stand, bedazzled and bereft of expression, as the R101 airship glided silently above the school glistening in the sunlight. "You may never see such a sight again," said our teacher. We didn't. The following October, and in a violent storm, the airship struck a hillside in France and exploded killing all but six of its passengers and crew. It ended airship construction in Britain.

Next morning during assembly the Head Master discoursed on the tragedy. "It could be a warning not to overreach ourselves in attempts to impress the world with our superiority." The few years spent at his school had witnessed many attempts to gain supremacy. The air, which had been relatively unexplored, shot into prominence when we won the Schneider Trophy in 1929, and the following year when Amy Johnson flew solo in an ill-equipped and flimsy machine to Australia in less than three weeks. Henry Seagrave set a new speedboat record and Malcolm Campbell broke the landspeed record in his "Bluebird." The "Flying Scotsman" and the "Cheltenham Flyer" broke records on the railways. Fred Perry and Dorothy Ward triumphed on the tennis courts and in cricket Larwood created a sensation with his bodyline bowling. These were all talking points at school and our young and fertile minds were eagerly receptive to these successes as proof of our superiority: a theme that insinuated itself into the school curriculum.

The final year at Hastings Road, in preparation for transfer to the Senior School, was spent under the tutelage of Mr Dainty, who also ran a tobacconist's shop with the help of his two sons in the Parade at Sutton Coldfield.

Mr Dainty was like his name; of small stature, neat, precise and of military bearing. He had close-cropped hair, always wore plus fours and spoke in a staccato manner. Multiplication tables and the elements of English grammar were relentlessly drummed into us. "They are absolute essentials if you are to obtain any kind of employment," stressed Mr Dainty, who also laid emphasis on a good general knowledge, and so we learned, with the aid of maps we drew round a stencil, the routes of the country's four railway companies, of the locations of coalfields, of the cotton and woollen industries and others that made us independent of any other nation.

There were some imports; tea, sugar, bananas and so on, but these were provided by our great and glorious Empire. Mr Dainty unrolled a map which he hung over the blackboard and indicated with a billiard cue he used as a pointer the red areas covering a third of the map. His Aaron's Rod was also used to give a tap on the head to the inattentive. There followed many lessons on the Empire "on which the sun never set". We were at an impressionable age and patriotism, or to be more precise, imperialism, was hammered into us on every possible occasion. The nation's glory and the invincibility of the British Empire were reflected in history and geography, instilled into us and echoed and re-echoed in poems, stories and songs.

Mr Dainty left no doubt in our youthful minds that we had been privileged "at heaven's command" to rule millions throughout the world because ours was the only way of life. "There is no other," asserted Mr Dainty. "God has chosen us to improve the lot of the Godless and lawless by ruling them according to our laws and converting them to Christianity. Ours is the responsibility to the rest of the world."

With hindsight there was an overabundance of indoctrination, but it gave us a sense of purpose without which we might have been left somewhat adrift. It was a theme not only repeated at school, but recurrent in magazines, comics and extolled on food labels and even on matchboxes. There were adventurous tales in the *British Boys Annual* and similar publications, of the British in far-flung outposts fighting against "tremendous odds" or "savage hordes" in between playing cricket. We always won but were humane in our treatment of those who had had the misfortune not to have been born white and British. None queried the God-given right to govern millions in India and Africa. It was the "white man's burden". We were unaware that the sun was already fading on the Empire, and there was a sudden upsurge of patriotism during the depression when we were urged to "Buy British", but none doubted that the Empire was a glorious and beneficent thing.

Just what the Imperial Enterprise did for the citizens of Birmingham in general and those of Perry Common in particular no-one seemed to know. The city's industries, we were told, flourished from the colonial trade. Half of the world's artifacts were made in Birmingham and, although the working classes seemed to gain little from this, there was never a doubt that the Empire was a source of glory. Empire Day and Saint George's Day were occasions for celebration, the singing of patriotic songs and reciting appropriate poems, and concluding with the lusty rendering of *Rule Britannia*, lest we forget that we held "dominion over palm and pine" and God would "make us mightier yet".

Nothing, it seemed, would ever shake the edifice that had brought manifold blessings to the grateful multi-coloured races in our Empire, which was understood by all to be the greatest ever known. It would never change except perhaps to grow and God would suspend the natural course of decay in our favour. Anyone who thought otherwise and had the temerity to say so was thought to be eccentric. In any case there were far too few of them to exert any influence and there was consternation when a strange man named Mahatma Gandhi arrived in England from India. He wandered around clad only in a loincloth and supported himself with a wooden staff claiming independence for India. His mission made headlines because he had fasted in support of his cause. People laughed and he was ridiculed. What was the man thinking of? Did he suppose that we should give away India? He returned to India a bitter and disappointed man and the incident faded into history.

We learned that there were other countries in Europe, of which we did not consider ourselves a part except by

171

a geographical accident. Events there were of little concern when we were proving our superiority almost daily. Such pre-eminence, remarked Mr Dainty, had not been achieved without cost and sacrifice, as we were reminded on 11th November when Armistice Day was commemorated. It was invariably a damp and misty day when drizzling rain fell noiselessly and dripped from the leafless trees as we were ushered by subdued voices into ranks around a hollow square; all of us, except the very poor, wearing a Flanders poppy. It was a solemn ceremony of undisguised patriotism. One of the masters recited:

They shall not grow old as we that are left grow old.
Age shall not wither them, nor the years condemn.
At the going down of the sun, and in the morning,
We will remember them.

The lines spoken with great emotion brought lumps to our throats. Mr Hinchley glorified the sacrifices made by countless thousands for King and Country that we might live.

There was no doubt that the war had been a terrible thing but no-one seemed to have much idea of what it had all been about. There had been fearful battles on something called "The Western Front" that had been heroically fought against a ruthless enemy. The singing of *Oh Valiant Hearts who to your Glory came* "brought a prickle of tears behind the eyes."

As eleven o'clock approached the atmosphere grew tense, so tense that you almost felt that you had been there living through that terrible slaughter. A bugler commissioned from the local drill hall sounded the *Last Post* and an eerie silence fell. Beyond the school wall all traffic stopped, factory machines were brought to a standstill, even trains were halted, and people stopped whatever they had been doing to stand in silence for two minutes. It seemed an interminable time in which to reflect on the dead, the wounded, the frightfulness of the Germans and the infamy of the Kaiser. The *Reveille* was sounded and the distant noise of exploding maroons recalled us from our reveries. We sang *Oh God, our Help in Ages Past* as thanksgiving to the almighty for having enlisted himself in the allied cause and trooped silently back into school.

The emotions stirred by the ceremony when the whole country fell silent were almost too deep for tears and, after the silence, the haunting bugle notes echoed in the mind. The Great War would not go away. Its long bleak shadow lay across boyhood. There were many fears in the late 1920s; poverty, unemployment, illness and premature death, but war was not one of them. There were too many reminders of the last one. There never would be, there never could be, another war: the League of Nations had made it impossible.

Each morning Mr Stackhouse, the Headmaster of the Senior Boys School, left his home in Sutton Coldfield to catch the single-deck Midland "Red" bus as far as Perry Common. Dismounting at Weycroft Road he turned in the direction of the schools in Hastings Road. With no traffic to soften the click of his precisely-measured footsteps the throngs of children swarming schoolwards parted at their approaching sound to allow him through. As a disciplinarian he was held in some awe, but he was kindly disposed, except to those who stepped out of line. He rarely resorted to corporal punishment. A mortifying flash over his half-moon, gold-rimmed, spectacles was usually enough to deflate all but the most persistent of miscreants.

The Headmaster had no secretarial help and he and his all-male staff managed all the administration and tutoring of boys aged between ten and fourteen. Each morning he dismissed us from assembly to the piano accompaniment of either Blake's "Grand March" or the "Robbers March" from *Chu Chin Chow* played by Mr Palmer, our class teacher, or Mr Clare, the music teacher, to concentrate on the three "Rs" and achieve sufficient mastery to pass the Grammar Schools Entrance Examination to be held in the following March.

For those who were successful there was only a slender chance that they would be able to take advantage of their ability. The cost of uniforms, books and fares, coupled with an extra two or three years at school at a time when there were no automatic grants proved insuperable for many parents. It was inevitable that a diversity of blossoming talent went undeveloped in the monotonous repetitive jobs many were forced into in the factories around Aston and Witton.

In a pre-metric age arithmetic was of paramount importance; its complications frustrating. We struggled with problems involving duo-decimal coinage, toiled converting inches, feet and yards to rods (poles or perches) to furlongs and miles; strove to change ounces and pounds to stones, pecks and bushels and then into hundredweights and tons, and transformed liquid measures from gills and pints to quarts and gallons, and all because the country had remained aloof from the metric system standardised in the rest of Europe by Napoleon a century and a half earlier.

English composition, grammar and spelling reinforced with dictation were pursued with frenetic energy, but there was some welcome relief in an introduction to English literature with readings from *Oliver Twist*, *The Tempest* and *The King of the Golden River*, which might seem rather advanced for ten-year olds. Elementary science was more technical than scientific. We learned to change a tap washer and mend a broken fuse, but there was also much talk about the possibility of splitting the atom and of pictures that might be beamed into our homes which would show events as they happened. There were visions of conquering Everest and of men rocketing to the moon but television seemed to be the only likelihood in our lifetime. The others were the dreams of explorers or fantasies in the imaginations of scientists.

The arrival at the school of a wireless set broke new ground in the teaching of history and geography when, on Friday afternoons, we were marched into the "wireless Room" to enjoy the novelty of the BBC Schools Service. The voice coming from the loudspeaker referred us to an illustrated pamphlet issued for use during the broadcasts and we learned of the Five Year Plan in Russia and of the Weimar Republic in Germany.

These were relatively unbiased broadcasts, and the pictures of the German people showed them to be much as we were. The Kaiser's barbaric hordes seemed to have evaporated.

The Grammar Schools Entrance Examination was held at King Edward's Grammar School, Aston, on a bitterly cold March day, but of those who satisfied the examiners only four or five of us were able to take advantage of our success. Lack of finance was to be blamed in most cases, but there were instances of prejudice and ignorance evident in remarks such as "What was good enough for your father is good enough for you!" and the urge to become wage earners at fourteen was so strong that it was practically an obligation if not a necessity. Dreams of going into long trousers, visions of a suit from the Fifty-shilling Tailors, the possession of an "Attaboy" trilby hat and emulating their fathers by smoking Woodbine cigarettes and going to the Villa on Saturday afternoons loomed large in the minds of most boys.

The offer of a place at Handsworth Grammar School created a dilemma. My father was determined that neither of his sons should be forced to work in a factory. "I don't mind what I go without as long as you and the boys are all right," he said to my mother who was more practical and pondered over the predicament. The journey to Handsworth would involve tram and bus fares on six days of the week (attendance on Saturday mornings was obligatory) and the cost of mid-day meals, plus uniforms and sports gear. "If we go without holidays and I take in dressmaking then, with what we have saved, it could be possible and," she concluded, "Handsworth is such a respectable area." What they deprived themselves of and how much they had to delve into their savings, especially when my brother joined me at the Grammar School, we never knew, but unforeseen help came from an unexpected source.

My mother, in her enthusiasm for the Co-operative Movement, had been elected to the Executive Committee of the Women's Guild in 1931 and came into frequent contact with Mr Edward Fennelly, the Education Secretary. He and his wife had become family friends and from them we learned that the Co-operative Society's Education Committee had recently introduced a scheme that entitled the sixty elementary school children who were placed highest in order of merit in the previous March Grammar School examinations to a grant of two pounds a year for four years. Whether I was one of the sixty or whether it was through my mother's work and her fulfilling of the "certain simple conditions" necessary to qualify I do not know but the forthcoming grant removed any uncertainty over the future.

I had spent only one year in the Senior School but it was a year filled with activity and interest and a happy year as new facts were revealed to us. Although the boys had been separated from the girls since the age of seven there was close co-operation with extra-mural activities. During the year the senior girls gave a creditable performance of James Barrie's *Quality Street* to which the boys were invited and the senior boys presented a variety show from which I recall but two items that made an impression; a selection of nigger minstrel songs sung by some of the boys camouflaged with dark grease-paint and some others purporting to be a group of Pilgrim Fathers who, suitably clad, carried lanterns to and fro across the stage singing *To be a Pilgrim*.

Grammar, Nonsense and Crises

Handsworth Grammar School for Boys had been founded a hundred years earlier with money left in the Bridge Trust Fund after its responsibilities for maintaining bridges in the district had been taken over by the local authority. It was a fee-paying establishment, except for those who had won scholarships or whose father's income lay below a certain level. It was not arithmetic that won me a place there, but an ability to spell and punctuate and a flair for English composition may have helped.

The first day coincided with that of a new Headmaster, the Reverend J.J. Walton, "Holy Joe" as he was quick to be called, a strict disciplinarian, who moulded his establishment along public school lines with all the traditions of school caps and ties, classics and culture and prefects and fags. There was even a school tuck shop. Our masters wore their mortar boards and gowns, the class rooms were form rooms, the playground was the quad and the assembly hall, for reasons we never learned, was referred to as "Big School". All the ingredients of "Greyfriars" were there, except that we were day boys and not boarders, and the prefects exercised an authority that extended to inflicting mild punishments for minor misdemeanours.

Suddenly we elementary school boys were catapulted, through the self-denial of our parents, into a coveted world we had only read about in *The Magnet* and *Gem*. The allocation to one of four "houses" created an esprit de corps that obliterated any latent snobbery towards scholarship boys by the sons from the more genteel strata of shop keepers, civil servants and bank clerks. We were all called, even among ourselves, by surname, with the suffix of major or minor where necessary.

After a nervous beginning we settled down to a learning that was solid but hardly adventurous. English grammar, mathematics, the sciences, arts, literature, history and geography were the backbone of learning. French was compulsory and there was a choice between Latin or German as a second language. There were many extramural activities to encourage us and stimulate our intellects; natural history, art, dramatic and operatic societies, a badminton club and an OTC (Officer training Corps). Sport, involving a two-mile walk to playing fields beyond Handsworth Wood, was compulsory, as was learning to swim at the public baths.

We were quick to respect the masters who stood no nonsense and to take advantage of those who could be played up or cajoled into recounting exploits that bore little reference to our studies. The chief sufferer of our conspiracies was a Mr Kenrick, an ageing bachelor affectionately referred to as "Gogs" but less affectionately subjected to subversive activities. He taught chemistry, which was rife with opportunities for chicanery with explosive mixtures and obnoxious-smelling compounds. His gown hung in shreds from his shoulders, a result of the exploits of generations of mischievous juveniles.

Mr Hutchinson (Captain when he took charge of the OTC) who taught physics, was an easy prey for side-tracking into recounting his wartime campaigns in Egypt and Mesopotamia. We wrestled with German declensions under Mr Gaydoul, nicknamed the "Flying Deutschman" because, unlike his fellow masters who progressed sedately along the corridors, he sped along with his gown billowing like the cloak of a vampire. He had a compelling enthusiasm for everything German and sometimes took time off from the intricacies of German grammar to read German poetry or play records of German songs on a gramophone he wound by hand. He did much to redress misconceptions of a blood-lusting nation.

The Head, as his cloth befitted, took divinity, but his homilies did little to increase our religious knowledge. His main concern — which amounted to a mania — was to improve our pronunciation of English. We had to repeat after him "The last master walked past, fast down the garden path" using the long "a" in an attempt to remove any traces of a Birmingham accent which, he insisted, would seriously damage any prospects of employment.

History ended with the death of King Edward VII and we were left in ignorance of the causes of the First World War. They had not reached the textbooks. Maybe it was still too near and none knew how to explain it, or the recollections of masters who had fought in it were too vivid for them to give unbiased accounts.

Two unanticipated bonuses were soon to be realised. Mr Hutchinson's anecdotes on Cairo came in useful, and my elementary German so astounded a soldier of the Afrika Korps that he refrained from shooting, lowered his rifle, took mine from me with a "Danke sehr," offered a cigarette and took me into captivity instead.

On the corner of Grove Lane and Soho Road on a murky December afternoon in 1936 a newspaper seller was attracting a small crowd. It didn't take much to draw a crowd; a woman dropping the egg she was carrying home for her tea; a little girl whose penny had rolled down a drain; but the paper seller's yells of "Royal crisis — picture of Mrs Simpson's babby" drew the sensation seekers. No-one had heard of Mrs Simpson but, by the time we had eavesdropped on conversations and over-looked the evening papers on the tram home, there seemed no doubt that Mrs Simpson, whoever she was, had designs on the King of England and an unoccupied throne.

The nation was stunned, the local population dazed. A small group had assembled at Mrs Murgatroyd's front gate where she was holding court beneath the flickering gas lamp. "They say the King might have to abdicate in favour of the Duke of York," she confided. "But what if the Duke of York don't want to be King?," queried Mrs Bright. Mrs Murgatroyd didn't know but supposed it would have to be Princess Elizabeth, poor little soul. "They'd have to do something about the Regent," squawked Mrs Lamoney. "Yer what?," said Mrs Murgatroyd, her mind apparently focussing itself on the cinema. Mrs Bright attempted to explain and suggested Queen Mary and then pondered "I wonder what she's really like, that Mrs Simpson?" "I'll tell you," Mrs Lamoney screeched "She's American, married and divorced twice. A prostitute, that's what she is."

This castigation stunned her audience into silence. "A prostitute doncha think?," she reiterated offering her poisoned chalice to Mrs Murgatroyd who shook her head and rejected it with a noncommittal "I dunno." Mrs Bright, her face a mask of perplexity, shook hers in unison, but Mrs Lamoney's flow of invective was not to be stemmed. "Shameless, that's what she is. They'll never stand for her as Queen — and you can laugh . . ." she shrieked, rounding on me as I passed through the garden gate with a grin on my face. "There'll be a revolution first," she predicted. "You mark my words" and, like Cassandra prophesying the fate of Troy, she promised Armageddon.

The crisis had burst upon us so suddenly that we felt we did not know the true facts and there were conflicting opinions. Most people maligned Mrs Simpson as a gold digger unworthy of King Edward who was a popular figure, but many blamed Mr Baldwin, the Prime Minister, for presenting the King with an ultimatum. Then suddenly, after a week of speculation and rumour, during which Mrs Lamoney continued to spit venom unabated, the short reign of King Edward VIII came to an end. Mrs Lamoney's prophecy was not to be fulfilled and, with a new King and Queen on the throne, she was able to return to her more mundane preoccupation

183

with the condition of the laundry that hung on her neighbours' washing lines.

At the Number Five tram terminus in Villa Road we waited to board the tram that would take us homeward one hot summer day and watched as the conductor walked round his tram holding onto a rope to turn the trolley pole and re-engage it on the overhead wire for the return journey. It looked simple enough. We determined to have a go and took seats on the open rear balcony on the top deck to conduct the experiment once the tram was underway. Encouraging each other in this reckless venture three of us seized the trolley rope and disengaged the trolley pole from the overhead wire while the car was in motion.

We had seriously underestimated the upward thrust of the pole. In our ignorance we had not even realised that it was sprung. Combined efforts to replace it on an overhead wire that swayed about above were futile. The situation was compounded when an older boy in his OTC uniform rose to help, smashing one of the little pink shades that surrounded an electric light with his rifle as he stood up. The tram ground to a halt and an incredulous conductor shot up the stairs. Snatching the rope he succeeded in replacing the trolley pole just as an enraged driver appeared. Names and addresses were taken and, with a severe admonishment that ended with "You'll hear more of this," we were turned off the vehicle to walk on our way.

The next two weeks were spent trembling at each knock at the door. Every click of the gate, footstep on the garden path and the flop of letters onto the door mat brought fresh terrors. Each night was spent on a bed of nails. Worse, the tram conductor knew which school we attended, and morning assemblies became nightmares of anguish. The sword of Damocles could not have engendered more terror. As the days passed and nothing transpired the fears began to lessen but the curse of Cain was slow to lift, and we had suffered so much mental torment and loss of concentration at school that never again was any attempt made to interfere with the progress of a corporation tramcar.

As the recession faded, apart from the abdication crisis and the death of the King, the years 1934 to 1937 saw a spate of celebrations. King George and Queen Mary celebrated their Silver Jubilee, there were several royal weddings and the Coronation of the new King and Queen. A copy of John Buchan's *The King's Grace* was given to the Grammar School pupils to commemorate the Silver Jubilee, and for the Coronation we were given a framed lithograph of the school.

At Perry Common there were street parties. People decorated their houses and lamp posts were festooned with garlands. Mr Appleyard, on his rent collecting round, frowned at some of the over-elaborate adornment of corporation property but wisely refrained from comment. School children were given a souvenir mug, a special tea and a tin of chocolates. Any babies born on Coronation Day were given a one pound note, and half-crowns (12p) were distributed to pensioners. An illuminated bus and a tram, radiating considerable heat, toured the city streets. The Dunlop Works Band gave a concert in Brookvale Park and the Tip Top Concert Party entertained in Perry Park. Throughout the city there were royal salutes and ceremonial parades.

We had become too sophisticated to join in the local celebrations but were not averse to watching others enjoying themselves, to watching the searchlight displays and joining the throngs in the City Centre to admire the decorations, where a lavish use of heraldry created a unifying theme. Banners, shields and coats of arms bedecked the buildings around Victoria Square, where an equestrian group depicting Saint George had been mounted on a column between an avenue of blue, white and gold standards. The smoke-blackened buildings along New Street, High Street and Corporation streets were camouflaged by banners and flags draped above the streets and bore the emblems of the Empire. At night the Council House, the Cathedral and Saint Martin's Church were floodlit. The columns of the Town Hall were strikingly silhouetted by lighting from behind and the new fire station was bathed in a roseate glow.

Behind all this window dressing there was, however, an uneasy feeling as the outside world stumbled from crisis to crisis. Hitler had set the alarm bells ringing when he re-occupied the Saarland; there were wars in Abyssinia and Manchuria and a civil war in Spain. Appeals to the League of Nations were in vain. There was disquiet in India and people shook their heads over Russia. There was talk of another war in Europe but no-one seemed to have any clear idea of who would be fighting whom, and Armistice Day continued to be solemnly observed. At school it was a moving occasion. The reading of the Roll of Honour beneath the stained glass memorial window was followed by the two-minute silence, the mournful lament of the trumpet of the OTC bugler and the hymns of gratitude to the fallen and to the Almighty for deliverance.

Despite apprehension over the future there was increasing prosperity among the population as the depression receded and most people had more money in their pockets than they had ever known. My father, promoted from his lathe to Superintendent of Trainees, found he had enough money to buy my mother a vacuum cleaner; a "Bustler" for five pounds, and an electric bowl fire that could only be used during the daylight hours because it had to be plugged in to the electric light socket. More pocket money was available for school trips to Stratford-upon-Avon and even to London for an evening trip for half a crown (12p).

This new-found prosperity gave free rein to the advertisers. Newspapers and magazines overflowed with publicity. Horlick's prevented night starvation, Craven "A" cigarettes were "kind to your throat", Kensitas gave away four extra cigarettes "for your friends" with every packet of twenty and Mr Therm, a Puck-like creature, beamed at us from magazine pages promising instant hot water from one of the Gas Department's heaters. The Loch Ness Monster appeared for the first time and has continued to re-appear ever since. It gave one of the petrol companies a splendid opportunity for publicity in announcing that its petrol would "knock less".

An increase in pocket money to half-a-crown a week

led to freedom on Saturday afternoons (we had to attend school on Saturday mornings) when I would meet Peter in town. After three years of surnames at school we resorted to Christian names to save any embarrassment when introduced to each other's parents. We had become great friends. Although some of our interests were disparate, it was an interest in happenings around us coupled with a subtle sense of humour that had drawn us together.

Discarding school uniforms and ties for sports coats and flamboyant, for those days, neckwear, the escapades usually began in the Rag Market chuckling over the antics and chatter of the traders and the dexterity of the china seller who grabbed a handful of plates, held them aloft and released them one at a time from one hand to the other without a breakage. "I'm not asking ten pounds or even five," he chirped. "Just give me twenty-five bob for this real Worcester tea service." Hands shot up and his assistant was kept busy wrapping up the bargains, while he dropped his takings into a chamber pot and prepared his next "amazing offer". The chatter and technique has not changed much over the intervening years.

Then to the Bull Ring to enjoy the free entertainment provided by the ever-present kerbside hawkers of catch-penny trash and brown paper carrier-bags. The narrow Bull Ring was so crowded on Saturday afternoons that it was a struggle to reach the top and the comparative tranquillity of New Street to explore Combridge's, Cornish's and Hudson's bookshops, which were narrow grottos with little room to browse and where the assistants seemed to be permanently engaged in ascending and descending ladders hooked onto a high brass rail to reach shelves fifteen feet high. There was an irresistible urge to buy the latest paperback for sixpence. The paperbacks were an innovation of the late 1930s; an enterprise of Penguin Books to make the works of classical and contemporary authors available at prices we could afford. The venture was so successful that it sparked off a new concept in bookselling, and the range was soon extended to include travel and adventure, biography and drama. Shakespeare for sixpence was well enough, but here was Shakespeare well edited and produced.

The climax of these expeditions was an orgy of tea and cakes. Boots teashop above the chemists at the corner of Bull Street and Colmore Row was the favourite rendezvous where we sometimes met other like-minded colleagues. We were of an age when everything and everyone amused, and the capers of the teatime music trio could send us into surreptitious convulsions. It had always been there, and the only difference between the performances and those of ten years earlier was in the repertoire. Strauss and Lehar had been superseded by Jerome Kern, Sigmund Romberg and Rudolf Friml, whose shows were taking the town by storm.

We did not often stay in town for the evening. The theatres and cinemas were too expensive for schoolboys, but there were other diversions from time to time. We never missed the University students' annual carnival torchlight procession, or the Onion Fair at the Serpentine, with its organs playing competing tunes and the throbbing traction engines that drove the cakewalk and the giant swingboats. There was always something to do and we never felt bored. Life was good in the middle thirties and the future seemed infinite.

There was little rebuilding in the city in the 1930s. The Co-operative Society, at its zenith, remodelled and extended its High Street premises. *The Times* building appeared at the top of the Bull Ring. King Edward's High School disappeared to be replaced by shops and the Paramount cinema (later the Odeon). Lewis's created something of a sensation by installing an escalator in the new Bull Street extension to the store. It was the first in the city and attracted so much interest that an attendant had to be stationed at its foot to regulate the gaping crowds, instruct those anxious to sample the "moving staircase" how to use it safely and to chastise the urchins besieging the store in anticipation of a free ride. A blue post box appeared alongside the red one in Corporation Street. It was for letters intended for the new air-mail service that was being introduced by Imperial Airways.

The trams and the increasing number of buses and cars had begun to test the one-way traffic system to its limits. Some modifications were made but traffic jams still built up. Crossing the road became an ordeal, especially outside Lewis's main corner entrance until Mr Hoare Belisha, a government minister, proposed the introduction of pedestrian crossings at strategic points, where "Belisha beacons" were erected on pavements and stripes painted on the roads. Priority was accorded to pedestrians who streamed across Corporation Street while frustrated motorists fumed in their vehicles and the situation had to be controlled by a policeman.

The confusion was compounded by the introduction of compulsory driving tests in 1935. "It's an insult to anyone's intelligence," said Uncle George, the only member of the family to own a car. He felt affronted. "I've bought a car and paid my five bob (25p) for a licence. There is no need to test my abilities. I am a responsible citizen," he declared vexatiously. His sentiments were echoed by many others who regarded the test with the deepest suspicion and its introduction as an interference with personal liberty. The inauguration of new road signs at the same time served only to aggravate the situation. "It is all extremely irritating and meddlesome," Uncle George concluded.

In an attempt to relieve some of the pressures we were under at school, an intrepid group of Fifth and Sixth Formers approached the Headmaster for permission to organise a dance. Other grammar schools held them to which we were invited. They were formal affairs. At King Edward's, Camp Hill, boys accompanying girl pupils had to be introduced to the Headmistress for vetting as suitable escorts for her girls. Appeals and entreaties were of no avail. "No female will ever cross this threshold while I remain Head," he asserted. "What other schools choose to do is their affair. It will not happen here." Thus the deputation was despatched and the subject never again raised.

Severe demands were put on us to strive for the London University Matriculation Certificate, without which we could only, we were told, "flounder around in life's shallows". Mathematics, geography and history were tackled with renewed vigour. Extra French and

German lessons were squeezed in on Saturday mornings and English grammar was superseded by intensive studies of Pope's *Rape of the Lock*, More's *Utopia* and *Julius Caesar*.

To counter this surfeit of culture we indulged in the lightest of contemporary reading, eagerly devouring the "Jeeves" novels of P.G. Wodehouse, the "Bindle" books of Herbert Jenkins and Richmal Crompton's "William" books borrowed from the nearby public library.

History had taught us to be alive to world events, and we were not unduly worried by a deteriorating situation in India or in Germany, but we were by the mischief of a rabble-rousing gang who called themselves Black-shirts, led by a disillusioned Labour politician, Sir Oswald Mosley, that culminated in an outburst of rioting against the Jews in the East End and provoked a violent demonstration in the Bull Ring.

Public indignation was further incensed by a series of scares and suspicion that a "Fifth Column" existed. It was suddenly brought home to us when a paragraph in the evening papers reported a police raid on a house in Erdington where they had found a schoolboy's bedroom festooned with Nazi publicity. They had come away with arms full of subversive propaganda. Here, apparently, they had discovered a sixteen-year old threatening the nation's security by distributing inflammatory literature. Worse, he was a Grammar School pupil; a fellow Fifth Former. We had known of his predilection. He had assailed us with his propaganda for some time and claimed to be in contact with Dr Goebbels. His claims were dismissed with derision and the whole thing was treated by us as a practical joke.

The reaction was horrifying. Not since we had been forced to witness a public flogging some years earlier, had there been such a sensational outburst. Hellfire spat from the Headmaster's lips. How many more of the city's schools had been infiltrated? For a week the school buzzed with excitement and speculation, then, like a pond disturbed by the throwing of a stone, the waves created ebbed to ripples and petered out.

We sat the Matriculation Examination in June. Some were over-confident, others despondent. I was philosophical and preferred not to forecast. The academic work was over but, with several weeks still to go before the term ended, the Devil stood no chance of finding work for idle hands. We were thrust into a round of end of term plays, a music festival, an art exhibition and a variety of interschool events to stimulate the competitive spirit. End of term had always been a solemn occasion. This one was to be even more so. Uncertainty over the examination results and apprehension over the future loomed. In five years there had been a joyous welding of friendships with boys from a variety of backgrounds in a secure environment that was about to be exchanged for an uncertain one.

We assembled in Big School. Five years earlier we had stood, nervous entrants, in the front row; now we stood at the back. The form masters came in and took their appointed seats on the platform. The Head read, as he had always done at the end of term, from *Corinthians*, Chapter 13. "Though I speak with the tongues of men and of angels . . . and understand all mysteries and all knowledge . . ." He droned on "Rejoice not in iniquity . . ." We knew it all by heart. The references to the putting away of childish things and faith, hope and charity. It had become wearying, but this was for the last time and there was a poignancy about it. Adolescent sentimentality took over and a lump rose in the throat when glancing at friends; some of their names soon to be added to the Roll of Honour. We joined in singing the School Anthem, the *Song of the Bridgebuilders*, appropriate to the original funding of the school:-

> On sure foundations build we God's new nations,
> Strong and clear tells each year
> Of new found relations

It was the last time we would stand there to sing:-

> To build together what none shall sever
> Bridges from man to man
> The whole wide world to span.

The Head addressed a few words to those of us who would be leaving, ending his valediction that we were "To strive, to seek, to find, but not to yield."

Thus we were dismissed. The school had given us what it had to give. What it had been unable to give we had to find for ourselves. The education we had received had widened our horizons beyond our real home backgrounds, but there was no going back. We had crossed the Rubicon and it had presented us with contradictions that were not easy to reconcile. There was a danger that our enlightenment could have resulted in a thin veneer of affectation but the humility learned at home prevented this. Our parents had not striven to give us an education with which to impress others, but to use to our and their advantage.

Towards War 1938-

The results of the 1938 Matriculation Examination were posted up at the Grammar School in July and those of us who had been successful could not get home quickly enough to relieve our parents of their anxieties, but no tram ever ground more slowly along Lozells Road nor bus halt more frequently down Witton Road. The Matriculation Certificate was the springboard to a university education that few could even contemplate.

For the majority, financial restraints precluded this. There were no automatic grants for university entrants and, consequently, the ripening of latent talents and skills went undeveloped and unused. The coveted certificate had to be an end in itself. For our parents it was the joyful evidence of a reward for their sacrifices. It was proof of a guaranteed standard of education for a pool of candidates suitable for employment in local government, banking, the lower ranks of the Civil Service, and for being articled to accountants, architects and solicitors. The possibility of becoming a barrister or of entering the medical profession was remote, if not impossible, for anyone with a working class background, and being articled to a firm meant that no, or very little, remuneration was forthcoming; the training itself was considered to be sufficient reward. Financial constraints inevitably resulted in a considerable waste of ability. Maurice was articled to a firm of accountants in

Waterloo Street and paid ten shillings (50p) a week for his efforts.

There was little career guidance forthcoming from schools and few working class parents had the knowledge or resources to launch their children into what were termed worthwhile careers, but most were adamant that their children should not be forced to work in factories as their fathers had been.

It was a time when there was great dissatisfaction over prevailing conditions in some of the factories which came in for especial criticism over the practice of taking on school leavers at the age of fourteen and dismissing them at eighteen when they became eligible for an adult wage. It was an iniquitous system used by insensitive employers to obtain a continuing supply of cheap labour that was not eradicated until the outbreak of the Second World War. It was a frequent topic of conversation between our neighbours whose children had suffered from the callousness of employers who seemed to be predominate among the smaller firms in Witton and Aston. Not all firms were guilty. There were some paternalistic employers who encouraged apprenticeships and adopted a more altruistic attitude to their employees and some of my erstwhile council school friends were lucky enough to find jobs for training as butchers or bakers with the Co-operative Society and one in a clerical job at the Society's Head Office.

"To get a good job you must be good at figures," was incessantly drummed into us at school and at home. It was not, of course, entirely true but dexterity with figures was of far more importance then than now.

Calculators were undreamed of and computers unimagined. Clerks and shop assistants spent hours adding up columns of figures and counterfoils of bills, and then transferring them to day books and ledgers by methods that had hardly changed over the centuries. Percentages, discounts and interest all had to be calculated without mechanical or electronic aids.

To my parents dismay I had neither interest in nor aptitude for figures, and my father prophesied that I would end up "sweeping the factory floor": a fate which seemed to be confirmed by his ability to transpose thousandths of an inch into millimeters, decimals to fractions and to use a micrometer, a slide rule and a vernier gauge or calipers with ease, yet he had received no formal education beyond the age of ten. His knowledge had all been acquired by self-determination.

The careers that appealed to me were dismissed by those who claimed to know better because they required expensive training (an architect) or had no prospects (commercial art). Mr Fennelly, alone among our friends who had received a university education, and, as Secretary of the Cooperative Society's Education Committee, encouraged me to go into the grocery business. "People will always need food," he said, adding with prophetic accuracy "even in wartime." I was not impressed and was later reprimanded for not accepting his advice more graciously instead of dismissing it petulantly with a "Not wanting to be a grocer's boy," but politeness is not, and never was, an attribute of youth. How could I have known that the food industry embraced prospects in hotels and restaurants? We never went into hotels, and experience of restaurants was limited to tea and cakes in Pattison's, Kunzle's, Lyons or Boots teashops.

No-one appeared to have any ideas of how distinctions in geography, art and English and a knowledge of French, German and history could be used to advance any career except that of teaching, which involved expensive training and, in any case had been dismissed by a former teacher.

It was a chance encounter with one of the library assistants in the local library that seemed to offer some prospects of a rewarding career, but the Matriculation Certificate was not enough. A competitive examination was held each autumn for prospective local government employees. Success in that was followed by an aptitude test to decide in which of the Corporation's departments a candidate was most likely to be useful. A medical examination and an interview would, if all had gone well, bring one to the brink of a promising career. The first hurdle lay three months ahead and, meanwhile, Maurice had his foot on the bottom rung of a career in accountancy and Peter had entered a bank. I had to do something until autumn. I presented myself at the Juvenile Employment Exchange in Margaret Street. Behind the counter a solemn-looking man sat writing.

He continued to write for several minutes and then raised his eyes, removed his gold-rimmed spectacles and peered myopically at me. "Yes," he snapped by way of greeting. I explained my position. Perhaps it was a mistake to say that I only wanted a job to fill in until the autumn. "Not much here," he volunteered thumbing through a drawer of cards. "Might try this. They want some sort of a clerk." He wrote down an address of a firm in the Jewellery Quarter on a piece of paper which he slid across to me.

I found my way to the address in a dilapidated looking building which appeared to have no entrance other than a door in a side passage. I knocked and pushed it open to be confronted by a burly man who spoke with a thick Birmingham accent. He told me that there was some clerical work but what he really wanted was someone to load shipments, of what he did not say, onto lorries for despatch. I surprised myself with my assertiveness and told him that the work hardly called for a grammar school education. He retorted by castigating the Juvenile Employment Exchange, the grammar schools and me for wasting his time.

An appointment at the offices of the Blue Star Line in Victoria Square was not encouraging and I declined a weekly wage of one pound and dubious prospects. The man at the Employment Exchange looked despairingly over his spectacles and mumbled something about not knowing what things were coming to. In his youth he would have been glad to have accepted anything. He made a few clicking noises with his tongue and suggested I might call again next week or, things being as they are, I might consider the Army. I thanked. him. He forced a faint smile and I came out dejected into the summer sunshine.

It was lunchtime and a trickle of clerks and secretaries began to emerge from the Council House and the Italian-ate offices along Colmore Row. The trickle became a flood of humanity dashing towards the nearby tram and bus stops or heading in the direction of The Churchyard (as the Cathedral Gardens were then called) or to Chamberlain Square to eat their sandwiches. I felt very envious. They were all smartly dressed; the young men in "Attaboy" trilby hats, the girls sporting millinery in the shape of pill boxes with a ridiculous piece of stiff veiling that half-covered their eyes or a "Robin Hood" style that had suddenly become popular. Such headgear could hardly be called hats. They were so small and perched insecurely forward that they obscured the vision from one eye and had to be restrained from falling off altogether by a band around the back of the head.

I had not had a successful morning, and the newsboys posters were further depressing. Hitler, having occupied Austria, was now rattling the sabre on behalf of the oppressed German minorities in Czechoslovakia. No-one wanted another war, which nevertheless seemed to be drawing nearer with succeeding crises. There was some mistrust of the Government and we felt we were not being told all the facts. Why else was there this huge rearmament programme? It was true that it was creating employment, but the fear of bombs and poisonous gas was uppermost in our minds. Despite the gloom, Birmingham went ahead with plans to celebrate its centenary of incorporation and we were treated to *The Pageant of Birmingham* splendidly staged against the back drop of Aston Hall, where stirring scenes from the city's history were re-enacted in an appropriate setting. The spectacle lasted for a week, overshadowed by international events.

The Munich crisis came suddenly in September and

we waited apprehensively as Neville Chamberlain flitted by air to and from the Continent attempting to appease the dictators. Sandbags appeared, were filled and hurriedly placed round the Town Hall, the Council House and other strategic buildings. Lewis's put on an exhibition of air raid precautions, which further depressed those who visited it, and an atmosphere of inevitability pervaded most conversations. Suddenly the crisis subsided as quickly as it had arisen. Chamberlain promised peace in our time. Everyone felt relieved although few believed him, but there was some satisfaction that one of the city's sons had maintained a precarious peace, and the following week when he visited the city he was accorded a triumphal procession.

The hastily filled sandbags were just as quickly removed and life returned to one of uneasy peace as harrowing tales of persecution reached us from Europe and refugees arrived in this country. The rumblings of unease and uncertainty continued as Hitler preoccupied himself proclaiming the superiority of the German race, which, after all, was no sillier than Britain's claim that God had made her mighty and would make her mightier yet. In the climate of the era it needed no great intelligence to appreciate our superiority. Conditioned as we were it occurred to no-one to think otherwise. If they did they would not have expressed it for fear of ridicule.

In October I passed the competitive examination for employment with the Corporation. It must have been self-evident at the next stage, the aptitude test, that I would be of little use in the Treasurer's, Tramways or any other department that demanded anything more than an elementary knowledge of mathematics, but I was invited for an interview at the Central Library in Ratcliff Place to assess my suitability for employment in the Public Libraries Department. I climbed the stairs of the old Reference Library, as I had done many times before with my father in his quest after knowledge, but never with so much trepidation. So much depended on this interview. A slightly-built man with thinning grey hair and a pleasant manner was greeting candidates at the door and directing them to seats. No-one spoke. We sat, regarding each other surreptitiously, in the cathedral-like atmosphere of the room where comfort and light had been sacrificed to the magnificence of Victorian architecture. The prevailing silence was broken only by the occasional turning of a leaf, the creaking of a chair or the sliding of a catalogue drawer. We waited in the Gothic gloom as names were called in hushed tones, so hushed that some had to be called twice, and we were ushered individually into the presence of H.M. Cashmore, the City Librarian, who selected his staff personally.

The interview consisted of little more than a rustling of one's application form, interjected with a grunt, a sniff or a peculiar high-pitched cough, which his staff quickly learned to recognise as a warning of his approach. He asked no questions and I did not have the temerity to ask any of him. I had been forewarned of his taciturnity and abruptness. The only information he volunteered was that unless his employees had passed the Elementary Examination of the Library Association by the age of twenty-one they would receive no increase in salary. He ended the interview without any indication of an offer of employment. Outside, the Deputy City Librarian said I would hear in a few days.

Two weeks later I became a junior assistant at Ward End Library for twenty three and six (£1.17p) a week. There was a great deal to be learned that was not apparent from the other side of the library counter. Much of it routine that is now carried out mechanically, photographically, electronically or not at all, but was considered to be absolutely essential then. The racing columns had to be obliterated from the sports pages of the newspapers to frustrate the bookies' runners and discourage them from using the library as a betting shop. Their nefarious activities had to be conducted surreptitiously because betting shops had not been legalised. All returned books had to be carefully inspected for damage and the removal of any hairpins, combs, chewing gum, and sometimes slices of bacon, that had been used as bookmarks.

All new books had to be checked page by page to see that all were present and in the correct sequence. A rigid discipline was enforced. There were no breaks for morning coffee and talking while working was discouraged; not only did it contravene the prominently displayed "silence" notices, but it was not conducive to concentration. Laughter brought immediate admonition from seniors and even a suppressed titter was sufficient to cause a frown.

Such strict routines were accepted with equanimity in most jobs, especially in the so-called professions. Punctuality and a uniform standard of dress were taken seriously. An excuse for a late arrival because of fog or a breakdown of a bus might be accepted once, but not twice. "You must make allowances and start out earlier," was the limit of sympathy one could expect, and one hot summer's day a youth who had the audacity to appear before the public without a tie was despatched at once to find one. Open-necked shirts were only tolerated for sporting events.

The following year, although it was to mark the end of an era, began with no immediate threat of war and I was moved to Perry Common Library. I was back on familiar territory and among people I knew. It was a happy period in which the autocracy with which the library system was run went largely unheeded by the Branch Librarian, Mr John Gilbert, who exuded kindness and tolerance, tempered with a rich sense of humour that infected his staff of three men and three girls. He did not shut himself away in his office as did most of the Branch Librarians, but spent much of his time among his staff, the cleaners and the public.

His example taught us much on the psychology of staff management that was to come in useful. The reaction of his staff was predictable. It was impossible not to enjoy working in such a cheerful and encouraging atmosphere, where laughter and morning coffee and afternoon tea were enjoyed, although strictly against the rules, even though we were expected to tackle many jobs which today would rouse the unions. All were undertaken cheerfully. We changed light bulbs, mended fuses, swept the snow from the forecourt in winter and mowed the lawns in summer, shovelled coke into the boiler house and stoked the boiler. Overalls were provided for doing the dirty jobs, the most undesirable of these was stoking the boiler that supplied the heating.

The boiler room was dark, damp, filthy and reeked with the sulphurous fumes from the boiler. When there were no men on duty the girls had to do the stoking. They put on a headscarf and an overall, covered their mouth and nose with a handkerchief and got on with the job. There was no question of going home if the temperature fell. You stoked a bit harder.

A van driven by Mr Slade (no-one would have thought of addressing him by his first name even if we had known it) called twice a day to deliver and collect books that had been requested by borrowers. Mr Slade was of a somewhat cynical disposition, but a cup of tea could reveal another side of his character; a bearer of news, a relayer of messages and sometimes gossip in an age when the telephone was strictly for business use only. All telephone calls had to be recorded on a sheet that had to balance with the quarterly account. Only in cases of extreme urgency could it be used for personal calls, which had to be paid for.

There was but one spell of gloom each week. It was the visit of the Inspector of Lending Libraries, Mr Grindle, who was charged with inspecting the administration, the buildings, the staff and the service. Mr Grindle arrived promptly at each branch on the appointed day travelling by Corporation tram or bus. If there was a choice then it had to be the tram because tram fares were the cheaper by one halfpenny and employees had to travel by the cheapest means and produce a ticket as evidence for reimbursement. By name, nature and apparel, Mr Grindle could have stepped from the pages of a Dickens novel. His cadaverous features, abrupt manner and dolorous expression of resigned despair struck terror into every junior and some of the Branch Librarians. He seemed to us to be very old and no-one could remember his predecessor.

Among his tasks was the passing of invoices for payment and approving the cataloguing and classification of all new books. If a branch librarian's ideas on the classification of a book differed from that of Mr Grindle, Mr Grindle always triumphed. His authority on classification was absolute and he was not a man with whom one argued. A junior job was to place a rubber stamp impression of ownership on the title page of each book. It had to be placed centrally and horizontally. This was initialled by Mr Grindle as proof that he had examined the book. If the impression was off centre or crooked detection was inevitable and the unfortunate junior responsible was sent for and severely admonished for slipshod work.

On one occasion a newly-appointed junior had the misfortune to impress the stamp upside down. Attempts to erase it with a rubber and a razor blade failed miserably. In desperation an effort was made to burnish the roughened paper and re-impress the stamp the right way up. The result was hopelessly inadequate and there was now no way of disguising the error. The unfortunate junior awaited Mr Grindle's next visit with trepidation and when called into Mr Grindle's presence retribution was swift. The offender's simple and truthful explanation of having made a mistake was unacceptable and he was subjected to an onslaught of chiding. He sought to placate Mr Grindle by pointing out courageously that it was only a cheap novel that he had desecrated. At this Mr Grindle took a sharp intake of breath and uttered his final condemnation "If you would stamp a halfcrown novel in so careless a fashion," he censured with rising voice, "so would you treat a priceless archive." His flow of invective was only stemmed by the timely appearance of Mr Gilbert to announce the imminent approach of the bus that was to carry him on the next stage of his journey.

Despite the monotony of some of the routine work, life was never dull at the library counter. Many readers expected us to recommend books in the belief that we had read every book in the library or, because they had unintentionally (or intentionally) left their glasses at home, would ask us to choose their books for them, and then there were those who expected instant recall of the titles of books they had borrowed previously. "I expect you remember. It was a book about a ship that sank. I borrowed it sometime last year." Some requests were easily satisfied; the address of a chimney sweep or the location of the nearest fish and chip shop; others required a degree of intuition. Requests for ordnance survey maps had to be handled tactfully. In anticipation of hostilities all maps had been withdrawn from the public shelves. Access to them was not denied but we were charged with deciding whether or not the applicant might be an enemy agent before supplying a map. Why did they want it? Were they looking for anything in particular?

Such interrogations were an embarrassment and as unnecessary as they were ridiculous. Doubtless the enemy had all the maps he required. This fear of spies was carried to even greater lengths when we had to remove all town plans from guide books and store them in locked cupboards.

Sometimes we were unwittingly led into dangerous waters. A request for an address in College Road from a young woman with a squalling baby in her arms seemed harmless enough. We had many similar requests that could be quickly satisfied from the Electoral Register. She perused the names in the column I indicated for a few minutes and then, with a triumphant shriek of "That's 'im," she swept out. She reappeared some half an hour later. "I want to thank you," she said. "His wife came to the door trailing half a dozen kids but, 'e's enjoyed the privileges of a husband with me and now 'e'll 'ave to pay for them" and, clutching her crying burden, she swept triumphantly from the building, leaving me to ponder over the probable consequences of an instinctive reaction to a simple request.

In contrast to the attractive libraries of today with their lively displays of books, records, compact discs, videos and coffee rooms, pre-war libraries were dull and sparsely-furnished with wooden chairs. Those who wanted to read the newspapers did not have the comfort of a chair. They had to stand where the papers were displayed on news stands. The rows of books on the shelves were, for the most part, uniformly bound and prosaic. There were no exhibitions, story hours, lunch-time concerts or anything else to tempt people to linger. Libraries were not places of entertainment but for study and learning, where the Silence Rule was strictly observed. Offenders were severely admonished and sometimes expelled for persistent rule-breaking.

There was an element of competition from the sub-scription libraries of W.H. Smith and Boots and the twopenny libraries run by enterprising newsagents. There was more than a hint of snobbery among the users of the circulating libraries who tended to regard the public libraries as "free libraries" for the working classes. Those who subscribed for their reading matter could borrow the latest novels upon publication whereas the public library users had to wait weeks, sometimes months because there was no way of reserving books. The frustrated readers had to be content with the senti-mental and outdated works of Warwick Deeping, Ethel M. Dell and Hall Caine or the adventure stories of John Buchan, Rider Haggard, Baroness Orczy or H. de Vere Stacpoole.

Detective stories were at their zenith in the 1930s and were in constant demand. The novels of Edgar Wallace, Agatha Christie, "Sapper" and Dorothy Sayers rarely reached the shelves. They were eagerly snatched at the counter from anyone returning them, and we would have been less than human if we had not surreptitiously put on one side those books for which some borrowers asked for continually. It was a risk we took and the con-sequences of such clandestine behaviour could have been serious.

The novels of James Joyce, D.H. Lawrence and others considered to be of a risque nature were available to readers who asked for them and who were considered to be "respectable", but such works were kept away from the public gaze in the staff workroom on a shelf unprofessionally labelled "Naughtyculture". Older readers read and re-read the Victorian and Edwardian novels by Florence Barclay, Conan Doyle and Mrs Henry Wood that filled shelves which rarely saw books by the authors who were rising to fame in the 1930s. The novels of Somerset Maugham, A.J. Cronin, Cecil Roberts, and many others whose names are not so enduring, rarely reached the shelves. They too were snatched as soon as they were returned. Young readers were poorly served. The junior shelves were lined with books on heroic exploits and adventure tales by Percy Westerman and T.A. Henty. They, and other books with a high moral tone, lay for the most part, undisturbed. It was the "William" books by Richmal Crompton and the "Biggles" books by Captain Johns that were in demand by the boys and the school adventure tales written by Angela Brazil and Elinor Brent-Dyer by the girls.

The policy seemed not to be one of what a book hungry public wanted to read but what it ought to read. Consequently every branch library had its quota of the essays of Steele and Addison, *Reflections on the French Revolution* and poetry by long dead poets lying undisturbed and gathering dust. It took a brave person to suggest the addition of a book reviewed in the *Sunday Times*. It might, if the Selection Committee had not already rejected it, be considered for purchase, but there would be a long wait before the book appeared.

The awkward and unsocial working hours endured by library staff restricted the times when I was able to meet my two greatest friends, Maurice and Peter. It was not often that we went out together. Maurice was forever sighing after his latest girl friend, who was always so much more exciting than the previous one. He claimed to have the perfect recipe for attracting girls, but it never worked for long. Likeable and full of fun, he tried too hard and then found he was rejected. It was a combined sense of humour and the ridiculous that had attracted Peter and me to each other since Grammar School days. He was so good-looking that he could have formed a liaison with any one of the girls that flocked around, but he treated them all with amusement. The idea of any permanent attachment was as unappealing to him as it was essential to Maurice who, after a rejection, spent hours in despondency despairing of ever finding the right girl. He never did. He was tragically killed during the last stages of the Second World War.

We were all apprehensive during 1938-39. No-one wanted a war and there were many peace meetings and movements but, with so much to do and enjoy now that we were free of parental restraints and had money in our pockets, we tried to cram as much as we could into any free time when money was not a prerequisite for enjoyment.

There was much in the way of free entertainment. Band concerts in the parks in summer and in the new Fire Station in the winter, and a comfortable seat in the re-built *Alexandra Theatre* could be had for sixpence at the twice-nightly repertory performances.

The theatres and the symphony concerts in the Town Hall were our main sources of pleasure during those years of discovery. There were few other places to meet in town. Most of the cafes closed early in the evening and public houses were not places where young people could meet without censure. In any case the few city centre pubs that were situated mainly in side streets were the evening resorts of working class, middle-aged men. Women were not allowed into the Smoke Room and only welcome in the Lounge if accompanied. No food was served and there was a stigma attached to those who habitually drank in pubs. It was a hang-over from the Victorian era when pubs were regarded as sinks of iniquity where decent respectable people were not to be found.

The only places where young people could meet with impunity were in the rash of milk bars that had sprung up in town, but even there one could not linger too long as there were always people waiting for seats to be vacated. The milk bars were an American idea where milk drinks in various guises and luscious ice creams were served in comfortable surroundings that encouraged trade because they opened directly onto the street. A decor of chromium and a bright expanse of glass lured people into an interior of high counters and stools where machines mixed exotic drinks beneath the bright neon lights of continuous lines of coloured gas that had superseded individual light bulbs. Milk bars in the proximity of theatres and cinemas were convenient

213

places to meet before a show and afterwards because they stayed open long after the cafes had closed.

Maurice and I rarely missed a weekly visit to the *Alexandra Theatre* where we saw many actors and actresses in Derek Salberg's repertory company who were one day to become famous. Peter was more impressed by the big London shows at the *Theatre Royal* and the *Prince of Wales*, and we made up parties. There was a practical advantage in this. The cheaper seats, which were all we could afford, could not be booked in advance and it was necessary to queue, sometimes for hours, for the Carl Rosa and D'Oyly Carte operas, so we took it in turns to queue while others went off to the nearest milk bar.

We saw all the lavish musical shows of Noel Coward and Ivor Novello with their spectacular stage settings and effects of erupting volcanoes, train crashes and sinking liners for a shilling (5p) by queueing for the gallery. It was unfortunate that there was a "closed season" for serious theatre-goers when the pantomimes were running. Pantomimes were so popular that the three largest theatres continued to play to full houses beyond Easter when people were queueing up in summer clothes.

Despite the fact that we did not always see eye to eye with our parents and rebelled against what we considered to be their old-fashioned ideas, life in the late 1930s was good for teenagers. We grumbled about the establishment and criticised the government. Youth at seventeen knows all the answers. Religion was a frequent source of irritation. We went to church less frequently than our parents would have liked us to. Why should we have to kneel down and confess our "manifold sins and wickedness?" What were these sins? Were they playing the wireless too loud or putting too much coal on the fire? And what was the wickedness? Was it staying out too late at night? Anyone out after half past ten at night was automatically deemed to be "up to no good". Despite everything it never occurred to anyone to leave home. Where would they go and who would feed them and do their washing and ironing and how could they possibly afford any furniture? People only dreamed of a home of their own when they thought of getting married.

1939 was a watershed in more ways than one. The Holidays with Pay Act had been introduced the previous year, which had meant that all but the very poor were entitled, not only to an annual holiday, but were paid to take one. Seaside resorts were filled to capacity by Birmingham folk during the first week in August, the traditional holiday week for the engineering trades, and trains to Rhyl, Blackpool, Scarborough and Weston-super-Mare were duplicated, with some triplicated. For many it was their first holiday and, as coming events cast their shadows before, they were determined to make the most of it.

By the spring Hitler was again on the rampage and with his armies already in Vienna and Prague Warsaw seemed almost certain to be next. Vague promises were made to support Poland in such an eventuality, but just what the British, or anyone else, could do with the distances involved could only be conjectured.

It was not only internationally that events were moving rapidly, but also at Perry Common. In the wake of an upsurge in private building in the surrounding countryside, and full employment, those who had been prudent turned their thoughts to becoming owner-occupiers. It was an unprecedented situation. Fifteen years earlier these same people had been grateful for the much-coveted council houses and to be released from terraced houses and freed from avaricious private land-lords.

The population of Perry Common had remained almost static throughout the years, but the centre of gravity had moved away. Since the building of King-standing, new shops with greater variety had been built there. The little wooden bank had gone and been replaced by one on the new estate, and the Women's Guild no longer met in the school hall. It had been moved to a new hall built over a new and bigger branch of the Co-operative Society. People now had to walk further and in different directions for facilities hitherto enjoyed on the little estate.

Another reason that encouraged people to think of moving was that any houses being vacated were being filled with a very different type of tenant from those earlier founders of the council house era. Many of those now arriving were being moved against their wills under a massive slum clearance programme that had been put in hand. There was resentment from those being moved in and disappointment among the original tenants who viewed the prospects uneasily. They had little in common with the newcomers who were being moved at ratepayers' expense and in vans in which their possessions had been "stoved" to prevent the importation of infection and undesirable livestock. The temptation to become "owner-occupiers" was strong, and we, and the parents of most of our friends, spent weekends inspecting nearby sites where houses were being built by local builders at Blakelands, Greenholm and New Oscott for around five hundred pounds. A deposit of twenty five pounds secured a plot; the balance being payable over twenty five years.

The houses were advertised as "standing on high ground in a healthy location and free from factory smoke and low-lying fogs". Our friends were moving away and into superior homes that had a front parlour (or lounge as the brochures described it) where they could entertain us separately away from the rest of the family.

Few of our original neighbours remained. Mrs Tebbs and her family, fearing air raids, had moved to the comparative safety of Solihull; others had gone to Sutton Coldfield or Ward End. Only the Murgatroyds, now bereft of their family, the Lamoneys and "Auntie Watkins" remained of the original occupants who had lived nearby. The Army had posted Mrs Murgatroyd's Raymon' overseas. She didn't know where but he'd sent a picture postcard from somewhere that read like the "Sewage Canal", whatever that was, and was crossing "Sarah's Desert", wherever that was. She laughed at her inability to pronounce unfamiliar words, but that was what they looked like to her.

Gladys, to Mrs Lamoney's chagrin, had defied all her predictions and was contemplating marriage to, it was

217

rumoured, a doctor. "It won't last," she forewarned, but she had little time to waste on Gladys as one of her own sons had anticipated marriage, and landed Mrs Lamoney in a predicament. "How could he do this?," she wailed. "They can't afford to get married," which was the only respectable way of resolving such a situation then. As for "Auntie Watkins", she had recovered from her eccentricity sufficiently to be almost humorous over "Mother" who had taken to her bed permanently complaining that she was having to wait a long time for the Pearly Gates to open. "The gates must have rusted shut," "Auntie Watkins" confided to Mrs Medding, "or Saint Peter has mislaid the keys." Mrs Medding, whose irrepressible sense of humour had endeared her to most people, suggested that perhaps the old lady's harp was being restrung. "Auntie Watkins" watched the exodus with envy, but she couldn't contemplate moving "Not while while mother's alive. It would kill her," she sighed.

The housing boom was accompanied by revivals in other trades and industries. There was corn in Egypt and the manufacturers of furniture and household goods were quick to reap the harvest. It was easy, claimed the advertisers, to furnish a house. There were "exceptional bargains on the easiest of terms". You didn't need money, the furnishers asserted. Deferred payments would solve your problems. You could furnish a whole house for a hundred pounds. Two shillings (10p) a week bought a three-piece suite, two and sixpence (12p) a dining room suite with a draw-leaf table and sideboard, or a bedroom suite in figured oak with a triple mirror dressing table. The temptation was irresistible for those who had put down all their savings into a deposit for a house.

A walk round these new estates superseded the erstwhile trip to the cemetery on Sunday afternoons, and interpreting the names given to their homes by the owners of "Mon Repos", "Chez Nous", "Dunroamin", "The Briar's" (with an apostrophe) was a popular pastime. It was not always easy. "Ersanmine", we concluded was a corruption of "Hers and Mine", "Millstone" was obviously named by someone with a wicked sense of humour. Completely defeated by "Cissald" we had the temerity to enquire of a neighbour who was labouring in his front garden. "Oh yes," he said with a grin. "Her name is Cissie and his is Reginald." The originality of the new homeowners seemed limitless.

The sight of a child relieving itself in the gutter was the final straw for my mother, who grew more distressed at the general deterioration of the surroundings and the disappearance of friends to fresh fields. It took some efforts to convince my father of the wisdom of buying property. He had always lived in rented property and saw no great virtue in depleting his savings to enrich the builders and building societies, but he lived long enough to pay off the mortgage and see the property rise over tenfold in value.

So we left the house we had outgrown and the once-compact little estate that had been swallowed up by the vast housing developments at Kingstanding and elsewhere and once again arrived on the edge of the city at Greenholm, where another little brook (long since culverted) ran through meadows that stretched towards Barr Beacon. Our new house was the last word in modernity; two reception rooms, a tiled kitchen, a bathroom upstairs with a hand basin; and there were three power socket outlets intended for an all-mains radio and a vacuum cleaner. There was no central heating system, but a boiler at the back of the dining room fireplace provided constant hot water in winter and an immersion heater in the airing cupboard did so in the summer. The house with its tiled fireplace surrounds was luxury indeed. There was no thought of ever owning a car, but space for a garage was provided. The road, street lamps and drainage system had not been installed when we moved in, but these were small disadvantages that would be rectified before the winter. The events that unfolded during the next five months prevented this for the next five years. The road remained a quagmire, undrained and unlit, except by the torches we carried at night.

As August slid into September and the traditional holiday season drew to its close the returning holiday-makers brought with them stories of delays on the railways because of troop movements as Hitler massed his troops along the Polish Corridor, a disputed territory since the end of the First World War. He bombed Warsaw, ignored Chamberlain's ultimatum, and the Prime Minister broadcast that Britain was once more at war after a brief interval of only twenty years.

The declaration came almost as a relief to us after the tensions and uncertainties of the past few years, but it was not greeted by cheering crowds as in 1914; rather with resignation coupled with apprehension. We felt that we had been deceived and that all the recent prosperity had been founded on rearmament. There was a brooding fatalism among the veterans of the earlier war. The horrors endured in the trenches during the "Kaiser's War" were too vivid, and their memories of those who had not returned were insufficiently dimmed for any enthusiasm. Their anxieties and disillusion with the war and its aftermath, of broken pledges for a better future made in 1919 that had not been realised, spilled over and perplexed a generation that had not known war, but was better educated, more enlightened and less easily swayed by propaganda.

We faced a dilemma of conscience. Disillusioned by the failure of the League of Nations to prevent the invasion of Abyssinia and stem the savagery of the Spanish Civil War we had lost faith, yet could not believe that the German people really wanted another war. We took issue with Maurice's father who insisted that the only good Germans were dead ones. It seemed incredible that a man of reason could think that way, but he had been injured in the First World War and probably had his reasons.

That evening I went into town with Maurice. It was out of sheer curiosity. Conversations on the bus were between confused and uncertain travellers who seemed more concerned with food rationing, the blackout and the interruption of careers than of fighting for King and Country. There was no talk of honour and duty. People had become more sophisticated and practical than at the outbreak of the earlier war and were more concerned

221

with the practicalities of hoarding food before rationing began in earnest. In town the sandbags had reappeared around the civic buildings and the cinemas had closed but all else appeared normal. No flag-waving crowds thronged Victoria Square and no patriotic songs echoed along the streets. "Birmingham," as the *Mail* reported next day "remained calm."

In the vivid imagination of youth we saw New Street in ruins and the remaining pillars of a fire-gutted Town Hall standing defiantly against a blazing sky. We fell silent and decided to walk home. A single-deck bus with darkened windows passed. It had been converted into an ambulance with stretchers along each side. In Perry Park anti-aircraft guns were being positioned in hastily constructed emplacements and searchlights raked the skies over a blacked out city.

During the previous week, when reality seemed to have been suspended, my brother was evacuated with most of the Grammar School and its staff, to Gloucestershire; barrage balloons enmeshed in wire rose to protect the city from aerial bombardment and glistened in the autumn sunshine; gas masks and air raid shelters were delivered in a frenzy of activity by officious wardens, gleeful to be able to exert some authority over a bewildered population that could only wait. During that week the good-natured Mrs Murgatroyd called with some mail that had been delivered to our old address. Refreshed by a cup of tea after her walk, she relaxed sufficiently to feel reassured that Raymon' would be safely away from any fighting. She lowered her teacup into its saucer and sighed with relief "He's in Singapore."

The gas lamps flickered at Perry Common and went out along the roads, and with them faded the last afterglow of the Victorian sunset that had lingered on through our youth. The events of 1939 had made a tragic mockery of the belief that the 1914-18 War had been the war to end wars.

Epilogue

It would be foolish to assert that there have been no improvements to a city that has been in a constant turmoil of rebuilding for the last fifty years. Once-notorious road junctions and tramway crossings that jeopardised traffic and pedestrians have been replaced by circuses on several levels that separate human from vehicular traffic and, in the city centre, there is more room to breathe. Flowers bloom and lawns and trees flourish where buildings were once so crowded in that no shaft of sunlight ever fell between them.

The Victorian grime has gone and with it many of the buildings coated by it; sadly so has much of the local character. The workshops, small factories, backyard foundries and forges that surrounded the city centre and earned for Birmingham the title "the workshop of the world" have all but disappeared along with many of their products that were despatched throughout the world to countries whose names have vanished from the maps; but the city has never lost sight of its motto, to which could well be added "outward and upward".

In an expanded city centre a plethora of hotels, restaurants, wine bars and nightclubs has proliferated as far as Five Ways and beyond to make an impact on a night life previously confined to the theatres, cinemas and a handful of dowdy pubs. Development continues at a pace undreamed of fifty years ago. The National

Indoor Arena and International Convention Centre have ensured the city's position as a European meeting place. Symphony Hall, home of a world-famous orchestra, overshadows the new *Repertory Theatre*, where *Bingley Hall* and the *Prince of Wales Theatre* delighted us in our youth. The Jewellery Quarter has been transformed, the canal system revitalised and a science park has been created in Aston. The Sadlers Wells Royal Ballet has been wooed to the city, and it is no longer a place where people come and then go again as quickly as possible. It has taken on a leading role as a modern city; a cultural centre for pleasure, tourism and business.

Solihull, Sutton Coldfield and other wealthy suburbs have become yet wealthier, the notorious slums have disappeared, and the Warwickshire and Worcestershire countryside has become commuter country for many prosperous citizens. The renowned National Exhibition Centre, an international railway station and an ever-expanding airport have put Birmingham firmly on the European scene. The city always seems to have got it right.

The core of the enlarged city centre remains; its principal streets follow much the same pattern as they did fifty years ago. Some thoroughfares have vanished altogether, others have been transformed into attractive pedestrian precincts where citizens can relax and enjoy the colourful floral displays. The traffic is much quieter; almost uncannily quiet; the atmosphere undisturbed by incessant traffic noise and unpolluted by choking exhaust fumes from rudimentary motor vehicles. The harsh intermittent grating of the bus drivers' gear

225

changing and the whining and screeching of the over-strained petrol engines labouring, overheating and sometimes exhausting themselves on the city's steep hills are absent. There is no earsplitting backfiring or spluttering from the crude cars and lorries that operated on petrol little removed from paraffin. The lumbering metallic clatter from the trams is absent and the clop of horses hooves no longer echoes from stone-cobbled alleys. The noise there is is of a more strident nature; a cacophony of canned "music" emanating from shops, each trying to outdo their neighbours.

Some buildings have survived, have been cleaned and renovated, others wantonly destroyed and replaced by ones that share a uniformity of architecture that lacks the character bestowed by local architects and builders upon the vanished ones. Concrete and glass have replaced the terracotta and blue bricks that once distinguished the city from all others.

The city that has emerged seems to be on an inhuman scale and is strangely uncomfortable to those of us who grew up in the old one. The once-cosy streets have been submerged beneath the ringways and expressways. The architecture is devoid of imagination and marred by lack of adornment. Only along Waterloo Street and Colmore Row is there a feeling of being "at home". Victoria Square, although changed, is still recognisable, but the tranquil haven we knew as Chamberlain Square has vanished for ever. People can still meet on the Art Gallery steps as in former times but they can no longer arrange an assignation "under the clock at Snow Hill" or at "Galloway's Corner". Both have perished. The tram lines have been preserved in Edmund Street but the trams no longer grind round the curve where a man used to stand with a watering can to ensure that it was well watered. The trams have long since disappeared along with some of the statues and delightful spherical gas lamps that once adorned the surrounding streets.

The Georgian and Victorian façades of the High Street and Bull Street shops that attracted the "carriage trade" have been supplanted by the concrete slabs of multiple stores and the streets distorted from their original lines. New Street and Corporation Street look vaguely familiar, although King Edward's High School, the Exchange and Royal and Grand theatres are missing and fast food restaurants and amusement arcades have replaced some of the quality shops. In a rebuilt Bull Ring, devoid of its cobbles and colourful barrow boys, and deflected from its earlier topography, a re-sited Nelson gazes on an ugly overpass that obscures the view of Saint Martin's Church.

Victoria Square, opened out by the demolition of Galloway's Corner, has been improved with lawns, flower beds and fountains. The Town Hall and Council House are shown to greater advantage than was previously possible because of overcrowding and traffic. The two buildings, restored and cleaned to reveal their respective Anglesey marble and red sandstone look almost unreal in their freshness to those accustomed to their pre-war grime and drabness. The intrusion of the new Central Library and ATV building to the West mars the scene and induces a feeling of looking at a familiar one through a theatrical gauze which one half expects to lift to reveal the transformation that lies beyond. It doesn't and there is a sensation, as Hamlet says, that "the time is out of joint."

The great railway stations with their magnificent overall glass roofs and enamelled advertisements for *Stephen's Ink*, *Virol* and *Palethorpe's Sausages* have gone. Snow Hill, where "Kings" and "Castles" roared in heading the cream of Great Western expresses, lay derelict for years. In 1977 what remained was demolished and a landmark that had witnessed every human emotion and been a meeting place for more than fifty years had vanished. Snow Hill had become but a name until, after discussion, deliberation and finally decision, a new station was built there to provide a commuter service. The station that was once the pride of the Great Western Railway has been replaced by one claimed to be more in keeping with the needs of today.

At New Street no stately "Claughtons" puff their smoke through shafts of sunlight towards the vast glass roof that once had the widest span of any in the country nor do any "Compounds" clank connecting rods musically on the "Midland Side." Both stations have been superseded by a huge subterranean cavern, tiled and clinical, where no daylight ever penetrates and an eerie silence pervades, broken only by the whine of electric locomotives and announcements in stentorian tones that echo through the oppressive mausoleum. Now that Moor Street too has been rebuilt nothing remains of the exciting stations that enchanted us in the 1930s.

The ringways encircling the old city centre may have solved the worst of the traffic problems but, for pedestrians, they have cut it off from the inner suburbs like the walls of a Mediaeval citadel. Penetration of these ramparts can only be effected through a maze of windswept tunnels, ramps and steps that, for the most part, are so filthy and infested with guitar-strumming buskers and muggers that only the intrepid will attempt a passage.

Of the scenes of earliest recollections almost nothing remains. The embattled tower of Saint George's Church with its crocketed pinnacles became a casualty to make way for the high-rise building at the top of Constitution Hill, and an inner ring road has cut off Wheeler Street as a main thoroughfare. Martha Place and its surrounding courts and corner shops have been pulled down and supplanted by a development on a more human scale.

Whether or not this development has been successful is a matter for conjecture. What is certain is that the motor vehicle has had a big influence in reshaping the city and the habits of its people. The old courts were units. People could relate to them and to each other. There was human contact in the sharing of the elementary facilities that brought a quick response to each other's joys and sorrows. In winter people cleared each other's snow away and in warm weather they brought chairs out into the courts and streets and chatted. Tradesmen came and went, horses clattered on the cobbles, trams clanked by and there were human noises; newsboys shouting, children calling, laughing and playing. The tower blocks and featureless dwellings that have replaced the courts are but a backdrop to a more sombre scene. Street life has become too dangerous.

Vehicles and muggers have driven people into their homes where they prefer to remain behind locked doors. Few walk, talk or shout. No faces peer from doorways, except in trepidation, and there is a silence, not of tranquillity but of apprehension.

Handsworth became a powder keg. It was once an attractive suburb of well-regarded Victorian terraces and Edwardian villas from which smartly-dressed housewives set off to shop along the Lozells or Soho Roads. The well-to-do from Handsworth Wood came by bus to shop in Villa Cross "village", a highly-esteemed shopping centre between the wars. There are few reminders of that ordered life. The shops now carry hieroglyphic signs and sell unfamiliar products. Their windows are protected with wire grilles and at night are shuttered with steel to deter vandals. Oriental beauties stare from cinema hoardings where once smiled Madeleine Carroll and Greta Garbo, Tyrone Power and Douglas Fairbanks.

The countryside that encircled the remote little estate at Perry Common has disappeared beneath developments that have engulfed even the Royal Borough of Sutton Coldfield. No longer isolated from the rest of the city it has all but lost its identity amidst the buildings and dual carriageways that have supplanted the fields and lanes. The little brook that gurgled and rippled through the meadows, the source of so much joy to us as children, was put into a culvert years ago and flows too fast for tiny fish.

The houses, their freshness weathered by time, have doubtless been modernised to acceptable standards and some probably bought. Front gardens, once carefully tended by tenants who vied in friendly competition for the coveted prize of the estate's best kept garden, have lost their fences and privet hedges to become hard standings for cars.

Along the roads the saplings planted sixty years ago are now mature trees beneath whose boughs the diesel-engined buses glide, power-steered, noiseless and smooth, between the lines of cars that fill the verges and spill over into the roads. No gas lamps hiss and splutter into life at dusk to flicker on the children playing in their pools of light. No crowds, thrilled by the latest Hollywood offering, emerge from the *Mayfair* to fill the air with excited chatter as they disperse homeward along the darkened streets. The cinema was pulled down after a brief but glorious spell to make way for a petrol station. The Circle shops have changed hands many times. The three Co-op stores, the mainspring of the beginnings of our social and cultural life, have vanished; the erstwhile premises appropriated by a superstore. The baker's horse no longer crops along the road each day at noon, and generations of children have passed through the school in Hastings Road since I was one of that first intake on a summer's day in 1926.

ISIS publish a wide range of books in large print, from fiction to biography. A full list of titles is available free of charge from the address below. Alternatively, contact your local library for details of their collection of ISIS large print books.

Details of ISIS complete and unabridged audio books are also available.

Any suggestions for books you would like to see in large print or audio are always welcome.

7 Centremead
Osney Mead
Oxford OX2 0ES
(01865) 250333

ISIS REMINISCENCE SERIES

The ISIS Reminiscence Series has been developed with the older reader in mind. Well-loved in their own right, these titles have been chosen for their memory-evoking content.

FRED ARCHER
The Cuckoo Pen
The Distant Scene
The Village Doctor

BRENDA BULLOCK
A Pocket With A Hole

WILLIAM COOPER
From Early Life

KATHLEEN DAYUS
All My Days
The Best of Times
Her People

DENIS FARRIER
Country Vet

WINIFRED FOLEY
Back to the Forest
No Pipe Dreams for Father

PEGGY GRAYSON
Buttercup Jill

JACK HARGREAVES
The Old Country

ISIS REMINISCENCE SERIES

MOLLIE HARRIS
A Kind of Magic

ANGELA HEWINS
The Dillen

ELSPETH HUXLEY
Gallipot Eyes

LESLEY LEWIS
The Private Life Of A Country House

JOAN MANT
All Muck, No Medals

BRIAN P. MARTIN
Tales of the Old Countrymen
Tales of Time and Tide

VICTORIA MASSEY
One Child's War

JOHN MOORE
Portrait of Elmbury

PHYLLIS NICHOLSON
Country Bouquet

GILDA O'NEILL
Pull No More Bines

VALERIE PORTER
Tales of the Old Country Vets
Tales of the Old Woodlanders

ISIS REMINISCENCE SERIES

BIOGRAPHY & AUTOBIOGRAPHY

NINA BAWDEN
In My Own Time

SALLY BECKER
The Angel of Mostar

CHRISTABEL BIELENBERG
The Road Ahead

CAROLINE BLACKWOOD
The Last of the Duchess

ALAN BLOOM
Come You Here, Boy!

ADRIENNE BLUE
Martina Unauthorized

BARBARA CARTLAND
I Reach for the Stars

CATRINE CLAY
Princess to Queen

JILL KERR CONWAY
True North

DAVID DAY
The Bevin Boy

MARGARET DURRELL
Whatever Happened to Margo?

BIOGRAPHY & AUTOBIOGRAPHY

MONICA EDWARDS
The Unsought Farm
The Cats of Punchbowl Farm

CHRISTOPHER FALKUS
The Life and Times of Charles II

LADY FORTESCUE
Sunset House

EUGENIE FRASER
The Dvina Remains
The House By the Dvina

KIT FRASER
Toff Down Pit

KENNETH HARRIS
The Queen

DON HAWORTH
The Fred Dibnah Story

PAUL HEINEY
Pulling Punches
Second Crop

SARA HENDERSON
From Strength to Strength

PAUL JAMES
Princess Alexandra

BIOGRAPHY & AUTOBIOGRAPHY

EILEEN JONES
Neil Kinnock

JAMES LEITH
Ironing John

FLAVIA LENG
Daphne du Maurier

MARGARET LEWIS
Edith Pargeter: Ellis Peters

VICTORIA MASSEY
One Child's War

NORMAN MURSELL
Come Dawn, Come Dusk

MICHAEL NICHOLSON
Natasha's Story

LESLEY O'BRIEN
Mary MacKillop Unveiled

ADRIAN PLASS
The Sacred Diary of Adrian Plass Aged 37 ³/₄

CHRIS RYAN
The One That Got Away

J. OSWALD SANDERS
Enjoying Your Best Years

VERNON SCANNELL
Drums of Morning

BIOGRAPHY & AUTOBIOGRAPHY

STEPHANIE SLATER WITH PAT LANCASTER
Beyond Fear

DAVA SOBEL
Longitude

DOUGLAS SUTHERLAND
Against the Wind
Born Yesterday

ALICE TAYLOR
The Night Before Christmas

SOPHIE THURNHAM
Sophie's Journey

CHRISTOPHER WILSON
A Greater Love

GENERAL NON-FICTION

Richard, Earl of Bradford
Stately Secrets

William Cash
Educating William

Clive Dunn
Permission to Laugh

Emma Ford
Countrywomen

Lady Fortescue
Sunset House

Joanna Goldsworthy
Mothers: Reflections by Daughters

Patricia Green, Charles Collingwood
& Heidi Niklaus
The Book of The Archers

Helene Hanff
Letter From New York

Andrew & Maria Hubert
A Wartime Christmas

Margaret Humphreys
Empty Cradles

James Leith
Ironing John

Lesley Lewis
The Private Life Of A Country House